WHAT THEY'RE SAYING ABOUT
FUN WORKS

"Fun not only works but is essential for healthy companies. It's not about *doing* funny things but *being* fun, something Leslie Yerkes has made perfectly clear in this very readable book."
    — Lena Andersson
       OD Consultant
       Lindingö, Sweden

"As a member of the board of the nonprofit organization I direct, Leslie practices what she writes about. She makes the work of the board much more interesting. Her book contains simple steps you can take to bring your whole self to work and grant permission to others to do the same."
    — John Colm
       President and Executive Director, WIRE-net
       Cleveland OH

"Leslie Yerkes' new book chronicles high-performing companies that create positive work cultures that drive out fear, increase risk-taking, strengthen trust, and encourage success. If you want your work to be like this, read this book. I loved it."
    — Dorothy Marcic
       Dr. Dorothy Productions
       Author of *Respect the Musical*
       Nashville TN

" Sometimes, we forget that work is supposed to be fun. Leslie's book reminds us how to return to the fun we have within us in a way that is good for business and good for our spiritual and financial health."
    — Mark Albion
       Author of the *New York Times* bestseller
       Making a Life, Making a Living
       Denver CO

"*Fun Works* should be taken seriously by any organization committed to success. It gives businesses compelling reasons to ask: 'How can having fun at work energize *our* productivity and profitability?' I'm giving this book to one of my clients."
> — Marilee Adams, PhD
> Author of *Change Your Questions, Change Your Life*
> Lambertville NJ

"I used to wonder how a financial-related business could emphasize fun. After reading *Fun Works,* I realized that fun does not necessarily mean silly or boisterous. I may not be able to express fun in all the ways shown here, but I do believe the workplace can be a place where it is fun to be and that work can be fun, too. I will consciously try to put into practices the principles of Fun/Work Fusion."
> — Donald G. Hart
> President, United Church Foundation
> New York NY

"It's not easy to get everyone at work on the same page. When it happens, it's powerful. Leslie's stories illustrate that fun can do just that. Fun does indeed work."
> — Steve Peplin
> President, Talan Products
> Cleveland OH

"Leslie's book makes you realize that when fun permeates the environment of an organization, it is irresistible, contagious, and automatic. When a company feels like a family, when you laugh, cry, and have fun together, retention is higher and growth is stronger and faster. But the smiles around the office on any given day are really the truest measurement."
> — Debbie Donley
> Principal, Vocon•
> Cleveland OH

"*Fun Works* creates the desire to encourage fun in any workplace. Leslie suggests that fun is not something bolted on as an afterthought, that fun at works comes only when fun is incorporated into your fundamental, everyday business processes. To every leader who wants a staff that looks forward to coming to work each and every day, I recommend *Fun Works.* To read and know Leslie Yerkes is to know that fun is always just around the corner and that without knowing it's happening, Leslie will pull you around the corner with her!"
> — Bret Brentall, Jr.
> President, Raritan Engineering
> Millvale NJ

ALSO BY LESLIE YERKES

301 Ways to Have Fun at Work
(with Dave Hemsath)

Beans: Four Principles for Running a Business in Good Times or Bad
(with Charles Decker)

They Just Don't Get It! Changing Resistance into Understanding
(with Randy Martin)

Business: The Ultimate Resource
(contributor)

Positively M.A.D. :
Making a Difference in Your Organizations, Communities, and the World
(contributor)

Motivation in the Twenty-First Century: Beyond Kicks & Carrots

∎

FUN WORKS

CREATING PLACES WHERE PEOPLE LOVE TO WORK

SECOND EDITION, UPDATED AND EXPANDED

LESLIE YERKES

BERRETT–KOEHLER PUBLISHERS, INC.
San Francisco

Berrett-Koehler Publishers, Inc.
235 Montgomery St, Suite 650
San Francisco, CA 94104-2916
Tel: (415) 288-0260 Fax: (415) 362-2512 www.bkconnection.com

Ordering Information
Quantity sales. Special discounts are available on quantity purchases by corporations, associations, and others. For details, contact the "Special Sales Department" at the Berrett-Koehler address above.
Individual sales. Berrett-Koehler publications are available through most bookstores. They can also be ordered direct from Berrett-Koehler: Tel: (800) 929-2929; Fax: (802) 864-7626; ww.bkconnection.com
Orders for college textbook/course adoption use. Please contact Berrett-Koehler: Tel: (800) 929-2929; Fax: (802) 864-7626.
Orders by U.S. trade bookstores and wholesalers. Please contact Publishers Group West, 1700 Fourth Street, Berkeley, CA 94710. Tel: (510) 528-1444; Fax (510) 528-3444.

Berrett-Koehler and the BK logo are registered trademarks of Berrett-Koehler Publishers, Inc.

Printed in the United States of America

Berrett-Koehler books are printed on long-lasting acid-free paper. When it is available, we choose paper that has been manufactured by environmentally responsible processes. These may include using trees grown in sustainable forests, incorporating recycled paper, minimizing chlorine in bleaching, or recycling the energy produced at the paper mill.

Set in Adobe Garamond and Ignatius ITC
Book produced and designed by Randy Martin, martinDESIGN
Copy editor Susan Martin

Library of Congress Cataloging-in-Publication Data
Yerkes, Leslie, 1958-
   Fun works : creating places where people love to work / by Leslie Yerkes. — 2nd ed., updated and expanded.
      p. cm.
   Includes indes.
   ISBN 978-1-57675-408-5 (pbk.)
   1. Personnel management. 2. Work environment. 3. Labor productivity. I. Title

HF5549.Y47   2007
658.3'14–dc22   2006034820

Second Edition
12 11 10 09 08 07   10 9 8 7 6 5 4 3 2 1

To all individuals who share their full selves
every day through their work.

CONTENTS

FOREWORD

I f I had to name the number one quality that distinguishes the most exemplary leaders I have interviewed," I said to my wife, Tae, "it would be *passion.*" I made that comment after a conversation in London with Claire Owen, founder and managing director of the SG Group, a 110-person firm that's a collection of four businesses designed to meet the marketing, recruitment, and human resource needs of agencies and corporations.

I first learned about Claire from a photo I saw in a business magazine. In the picture were people covered in mud, driving all-terrain vehicles and riding in tanks. The accompanying article reported, in part, "Twice a year, Stopgap (a company in the SG Group) takes its employees on unconventional outings, such as rappelling in Switzerland or making sci-fi movies in the London suburbs. . . Why? Because company picnics just aren't memorable enough, says co-founder Claire Owen." I had to meet this woman!

When I interviewed Claire on the phone and met her in person, the video and the audio were in synch. You get this electric feeling when you're with Claire. She exudes passion for the business and a deep caring for her team members, their candidates, and their clients. I felt energized and elevated after being with her for just a few minutes. It wouldn't surprise any of the readers of this book that the SG Group possesses as many of the eleven Fun Work Principles. Fun-loving, passionate people are just going to make better leaders than nononsense, unenthusiastic types who have no place for a bit of foolishness in their lives.

But, I have to qualify my earlier statement. Passion may be the dividing line between good and great, but it's not all there is to leadership. Among the other attributes one needs is *compassion.* Too much passion and too much energy can overwhelm other people. They can also stifle engagement and dissent. Passion and energy can be found among ruthless dictators and overbearing bosses. To balance their ardent enthusiasm for the cause, the best leaders need an equal amount of love for those whom they lead and an unrestrained desire to see them grow, develop, and be in charge of their own lives. Not only do you see this in Claire Owen, but you also see it in one way or another in every leader mentioned in *Fun Works*. It's this combination of passion and compassion that makes the companies in Leslie's book enjoyable places to work.

Fun to Leslie is not just about the lighter side of work, the most common connotation the word has. To Leslie, fun is about something much more profound. It's about the sum total of the qualities that create a sense of community. Community may not be the stuff of ordinary organizations, but it is the stuff of great ones, ones with strong cultures. The best leaders know that every gathering of a group is a chance to renew commitment. They know that every moment at work is a chance to make sure that everyone knows why they're all there and how they're going to act in service of that purpose. They know that trust, expansive thinking, authenticity, and choice — all topics of discussion in *Fun Works* — are critical to success and significance.

In *Fun Works* you'll read about some uniquely fascinating places. Some you might expect, such as the Pike Place Fish market made famous in print and on television for its fish-tossing antics, and Southwest Airlines, known to all of us who fly for great service and humorous flight attendant commentary. Others you won't, such as Harvard University Dining Service, where you'll see how they took a formerly staid commodity-driven service and created visually delicious and visually appealing fare for hungry college students. Or there's American Skandia, a manufacturer and wholesaler of insurance and financial planning products and services. Fun isn't exactly the first word that comes to mind when you hear the word insurance, but American Skandia has found ways to celebrate all the time with the Holiday Tree, Blue Fish ball games, Warm Fuzzies, and lots of other innovative ways to recognize exemplary performance.

Fun Works is a wonderfully written book. It has everything a business book reader wants. Solid principles, excellent stories to illustrate the point, and action tips about putting each into practice. You can even take the "Fun/Work Fusion Inventory" to test your own fun quotient and see if you're still in the horse and buggy days or are now up with the times, of bringing your whole self to work. And with this updated version, Leslie even follows up on the original stories to bring us current with each case example.

You might be tempted to hide this book in your briefcase for fear that your boss might think you're trying to figure out creative ways to goof off at work. Instead, I recommend that you place it proudly on the top of your desk for all to see, letting them know that you are serious about creating a place where people love to work.

Jim Kouzes
The Leadership Challenge

■

PREFACE

It seems as though every day I see the word 'fun' in a headline; I see it in newspapers, in magazines, in correspondence, and on billboards. In my job as a change management consultant, I hear people talking about it during their workday. I hear it on the radio, on TV, and in the lyrics to songs. From what I hear and what I read, not only are we interested in fun, we are hungry for it.

If we are hungry for fun, we are *starved* for fun at work!

You and I spend more time at work than at any other single activity in our lives. Yet, often our work experience is not fun. We suffer from the lack of integration of fun and work. The intention of *Fun Works* is to challenge our feelings and beliefs that:

- **Fun should exist only after the work is completed,**
- **Fun is silly, superficial, and unprofessional;**
- **Fun is taboo in the workplace.**

Fun Works is also designed to illustrate vividly that there are many people (and entire companies) who daily experience the joy of fun at work while creating impressive results.

In 1996, Dave Hemsath, who sells business books for a living, told me that customers repeatedly told him they wanted to buy books about fun and work but there weren't any. At that point, the two of us determined we would each fill one of our personal goals in life: write a book; but that we would do it together. We decided that our first (and maybe our *only*) book would be about the things people did to make work fun; about the fun things they did to have fun at work.

The result was *301 Ways to Have Fun at Work,* a happy little book filled with tips, tools, ideas, and examples to spice up your work with fun. That people continue to thirst for more fun at work is witnessed by the fact that *301 Ways* has sold more than 75,000 copies and has been translated into ten languages.

To support that book, I traveled throughout America and Europe, speaking on having fun at work. During those travels, I discovered how universal the collective desire for fun at work truly is. And I discovered that my consulting interest was turning from *doing* fun things to *being* fun. I discovered I was less interested in learning things people did that were fun, and more interested in finding people who integrated fun and work on a daily basis and analyzing what results that combination produced.

Over the course of 2000, I began to research companies that were known for their successful integration of fun and work. From my original list of nearly one thousand potential target companies, I chose three dozen to research further, eventually whittling the list down to eleven to represent the eleven principles of the Fun/Work Fusion.

In this second edition of *Fun Works*, I have chosen to let the stories of each company stand as originally presented in the first edition. I made this decision for several reasons. First, I feel the original stories are still 100% valid and present perfectly to the reader the principles each company represents. No modification is required; the original case is well-served. Second, I wanted readers to be able to make his or her own judgment on the change and growth of each of our Living Laboratories and determine for themselves whether or not they feel the company has lived up to its original role-model status.

Following each original story is an update, an extension of the original case study, which evaluates and analyzes the level of success each company has experienced over the last six years. Following that is a key which illustrates how to apply the principle.

One of the inherent problems in creating a list of the best of anything is seeing how well that list weathers the test of time. Will a company, once elevated to role-model status, sustain its validity and authenticity and grow? Or, will it stagnate? Even fail? And if it should decline, what are the causes?

As anyone who is or has been in business for themselves knows, it is very difficult to find and/or create new business for an organization; and once found or created, even more difficult to keep it. Creating an organization worthy enough to be chosen for any list of outstanding examples is difficult; staying there is seemingly next to impossible.

That being said, I was thrilled to discover that *all* of our original eleven companies prospered and grew; that not one of them was 'done in' by having a culture of 'fun at work.' I, of course, believe that it is *precisely* the culture of 'fun at work' that allowed them to maintain their position, stay in business, and grow.

With these slight modifications.

One Prudential Exchange (Hire Good People and Get Out of the Way) was technically not a company. It was a program created by Prudential to help change its culture. You will discover in reading this second edition that OPX, as it is known, did its job splendidly and was subsequently retired. As a result of OPX, Prudential has grown tremendously. I think this qualifies as proving the point.

Because of its good-company qualities, American Skandia (Celebrate) was purchased in 2003 by the very same Prudential and exists today as a division called Prudential-American Skandia, its culture still intact.

Employease (Trust the Process) was purchased by ADT in the summer of 2006 after a two-year business-project partnership with ADT because of its good-company qualities and the positive, mutual working relationship they both experienced. As of this writing, the naming status is undecided but Employease's personnel and culture will remain in place.

Finally, Will Vinton Studios had a failure of hard science and was purchased by Phil Knight, co-founder of Nike Corporation. Employees of the newly named Laika Entertainment indicate the Will Vinton Studios culture remains largely in place. Will himself has started a new venture, Freewill Entertainment. He promises to focus more strongly on the hard science of finance while continuing to maintain his commitment to the soft science culture of fun at work. Both studios continue to produce outstanding, high-level, animated products.

Clearly, the companies chosen to represent the principles of the Fun/Work Fusion in 2000 were good choices. In the ensuing 6 years, these companies have grown and prospered in spite of national tragedies, natural disaster, growing competition, and changing economic conditions. It is my thesis that they have done so because of the culture they created through The Fun/Work Fusion.

My original research showed: fun was not merely activities applied to the work situation, but rather a way of being; fun, when most effective, was not *input* but rather *output*; fun did not create a good work place so much as a good work place created fun.

During these last six years, I have come to reframe my discussion of Fun/Work Fusion to talk about the culture of a company. Creating places where people love to work is about creating a culture where individuals can freely bring the best of their whole selves to work each day. It is my belief that the resiliency and sustainability the eleven case companies have demonstrated over the last six years can be attributed to the successful interactions of these two things: business smarts and a positive culture. I call these two things hard science and soft science, and think of them as the Yin and Yang of sustainable organizations.

Hard science deals with great product, good strategy, continuous improvement, service orientation, strict fiscal management, and a vision that embraces the ever-changing business environment.

Soft science is about the people, their interactions with and relationship to their individual work and to each other — the culture of the organization. People make the hard science work, or *not* work; they make the organization shine or simply get by.

To be successful, an organization must first have powerful hard science. To be sustainable, hard science must be supported by effective soft science. Hard and soft science are equally important — both must exist to create sustainable organizations. Soft science, however, ultimately differentiates and contributes the most toward long-term, sustainable success.

I believe that the single-most important factor in producing sustainable organizations is the creation and development of effective soft science through the use of The Fun/Work Fusion.

I think the Living Laboratory companies in *Fun Works* prove this thesis.

What will *Fun Works* do for you? *Fun Works* will provide you with principles that, if applied successfully, will help you integrate your work with fun, sustain an engaging culture, and develop effective soft science. When fun and work are once again fully integrated in your organization, you will work enthusiastically, enjoy the process, and recover more fully during your time away from work.

The title of this book is itself the simplest benefit statement: fun works. If you follow these eleven principles and *be* them, then fun works. The title is also an aspiration: Can I create a place, a Fun Works, Inc., that produces quality products and services, creates enduring internal and external relationships, and is known for its culture of fun?

If I can, then fun works.

How we think about work is not a constant, it changes. We are now beginning to think about the integration of fun and work and we are beginning to demand working conditions that have an acceptable blend of fun and work. It's time to talk about fun at work and to raise it to a higher plane, to make fun at work important once again. I hope that *Fun Works* will be able to help you do just that.

It is my belief, and I hope it becomes yours — fun works.

Leslie

Leslie Yerkes
Cleveland, Ohio
February 2007

■

PART ONE
Creating the Fun/Work Fusion

"If a man insisted always on being serious, and never allowed himself a bit of fun and relaxation, he would go mad or become unstable without knowing it."

HERODOTUS

INTRODUCTION
The Case for Integrating Fun and Work

Anyone who's worked with contractors on a building project has a story; usually it's a horror story. Contractors, these stories go, are a real pain. They tell you one thing and do another; they substitute materials; they move tradespeople arbitrarily from one job to another so there's no continuity on your project. In short, working with contractors is not fun. Or so the stories go.

My experience, however, is 180° different. My contractor story is a fun one and the payoff, the final product, is award-winning. And it's different because in my story the contractors had fun at work.

It took me two years to find the right space for my new office. For the first five years of my business, I worked from my home (like many entrepreneurs) creating a very successful and profitable change-management consulting practice. Now I wanted to have my own, separate office space — a space in which I could have employees and clients and fun.

My requirements for this space included being downtown on the ground floor with floor-to-ceiling windows that looked out on trees — not an easy task in Cleveland, Ohio. But I persevered. The space I eventually found was connected to a city park and had the windows I needed. Inside the space, however, were rooms and walls and doors. Because of the kind of the business I'm in, one that places high value on the free flow of ideas and information, I wanted a special space that would embody those principles. To me, that meant it had to have no rooms, no offices, no head-of-the-table, no hierarchy.

Fortunately, Bill Mason, the architect who was assigned to me by the building owner, understood my ideas and was able to develop my vision into a physical reality. The successful birth of my new office space depended on the creation of a good plan, and the plan that Bill created was perfect. All we needed to be successful now was a good midwife. We needed a contractor.

Because this was my first 'real' office space, and because it was a unique, non-traditional design, and because I'm a naturally involved and enthusiastic person (some even call me a Hokey-Pokey Person but that's another story), I visited the site twice daily; once in the morning to ask the contractor and tradespeople what was planned for the day, and once in the evening to check on the progress. Because my work with clients deals constantly with organizational development, I was acutely aware that everyone works better when someone's interested in what they're doing and when they're praised for their performance and their results. I was prepared to provide that.

At the end of one working day, as the space changed from wires and nails and dust into something that began to resemble the dream I had in my head of my new work home, I found myself really excited with the day's results. I was filled with exuberance and sudden, uncontrollable energy and, like some character from a Jules Fieffer cartoon, I decided to do 'A Dance of Done Well.' But instead of just performing this impromptu jig by myself I asked the three contractors present to join me. And somewhat to my surprise, they did.

Visualize one blonde lady in a dress, a man wearing paint-spattered bib overalls, and two men in jeans with tool belts around their waists holding hands and dancing in a circle. You now have a picture of 'The Dance of Done Well.'

Over the course of the next several weeks, this impromptu experience developed into a ritual. In the mornings, I would meet with the craftsmen onsite and discuss what they were going to accomplish that day; in the evenings we would celebrate their accomplishments with a dance. If the day's project was drywall, for example, in the evening we celebrated with 'The Dance of Drywall Done Well.' The days that followed became a lot of fun for everyone involved. The work of the day was enthusiastically anticipated by each tradesman and results were at the highest level of accomplishment. Because of these daily dances, each individual contractor and craftsman strove to do their best work — work that would be worthy of a dance of celebration. The space was becoming my dream.

Finally, the office was completed enough for me to move in but, as in many building experiences, there were still a few last-minute details to be handled. On this particular day, two seasoned and highly conservative electricians showed up to install the gallery-style lighting for the sculpture that was commissioned for our office. I explained to them why the sculpture was important to me and our company, what it represented, and how I envisioned this work of art affecting the clients who came into our space. The two men understood and declared that they'd give the project their utmost attention, and then they said to me, "You aren't going to make us dance, are you?"

I was amazed. In the contracting community in Cleveland, I had apparently become known as 'the lady who makes you dance.' I smiled and laughed and told them I wouldn't make them dance but asked them if it was okay if I got excited when they were done. They allowed as that would be all right and went to work.

By noon they had finished and I inspected their work and they showed me how the switches worked and how to change the bulbs when they burned out, no easy task in a space with 14-foot ceilings! I thanked them profusely and shook their hands. This was the point at which I expected them to leave. They had performed their best work and they had been praised for it. All the structures and requirements of the work relationship had apparently been fulfilled. Instead, they stood at the door, silent and expectant, looking alternately at their work and at me. After several seconds of this waiting, one of them looked me in the eye and said, "Aren't you going to ask us to dance?"

I had discovered an essential truth about what makes work valuable: Work Needs Fun. If there isn't fun in work, if there isn't enjoyment, work doesn't mean as much to the workers.

So, what did we do? We danced.

THE FUSION OF WORK AND FUN we experienced while building my new office space created a working relationship which all the members of the process valued highly. Not only was it a peak experience for the individuals involved, but the outcome of our work created a peak result: the space was gorgeous. The reality exceeded my dreams. Together, we had created something greater than the sum of its parts. The fusion of fun and work also has bottom-line value: our office space was awarded the AIA Ohio Design Award of Honor and the IBD-CID Award of Merit. To my way of thinking, these awards are the visible, tangible, outside confirmation that fun works. And it works well!

My new space also allowed me to attract and retain employees and clients whose values were in alignment with mine. Because my workspace so perfectly represented my energy and values, people who entered it for the first time would immediately feel comfortable and energized themselves — or they wouldn't! Either way, I now had a first-line screening tool to help me select people who would best improve my business.

My contractor story is one example of how when fun and work are successfully integrated both the process and the resultant product are improved.

IF WORK AND FUN ARE BEST WHEN integrated, how did we get to the current state where the common perception is that fun is an add-on? That the only *time* we are allowed to have fun is *after* work is over; that the only *way* we can have fun is to *earn* it through hard work? Work hasn't always been perceived in this way; work and the perception of work have changed and evolved. As you can see from The Timeline of Work Attitudes, work has evolved from Aristotle's 'work is for slaves' to Calvin's 'work is a commandment;' from 'work is a virtue' to 'work is who I am.'

We adopt the attitude toward work that our parents taught us; or we assimilate the attitude currently held by the strongest influence: our peer group or our employer. For many of us, work has become who we are. It is how we define ourselves. Unfortunately, that often means that work is life without fun, without friends, without family. In *The Working Life: The Promise and Betrayal of Modern Work*, Joanne B. Ciulla says "…work sometimes substitutes for the fulfillment we used to derive from family, friends, religion, and community…. One of the first things Americans do when they meet someone new is say, 'What do you do for a living?'"

Regardless of where society happens to be on the work-life timeline, it is possible to intentionally adopt individual elements into the current prevailing attitudes. Specifically, it is possible to reintegrate fun into our work. I say reintegrate because for long periods of time fun and

THE TIMELINE OF WORK ATTITUDES

BEN FRANKLIN

Advocates work as a virtue; not a means to amass wealth but as a contribution of self. America is the land of opportunity. Work becomes the key to wealth.

THE TRADES

Working with your hands as a skilled artisan is highly prized. Payment provided for work. With the onset of the Renaissance, work and art are merged.

CALVIN & LUTHER

Work as a commandment and moral obligation. The evolution of the Protestant Work Ethic.

EARLY GREEKS

Focus not on work but on personal development. Work was completed by those enslaved. The emergence of the concept of 'liberal arts,' and the pursuit of knowledge.

CRAFTSMEN VS PROFESSIONALS

Separation between people who work with their hands and professionals who work with their heads. The bias is that working with your head is a more esteemed vocation.

UNIONS

Unions help workers defend their ability to earn a livelihood against managers and owners who see employees as objects.

1990s

Empowerment, Building the Team, and Reengineering begin the decade. Downsizing at the end of the decade completes the near total loss of loyalty as an organizational value.

2000s

Because we spend more time at work than at any other activity, we begin to question whether we live to work or work to live. The beginning of the Fun/Work Fusion.

1950s

The beginning of understanding of the culture of work in terms of Theory X and Theory Y.
    Loyalty to the organization becomes the expected norm.

1970s

Democracy comes to the workplace. Sexes and races begin to assume more equal roles in all aspects of work environments.

1980s

Gurus abound. How to make work meaningful. TQM becomes the newest program of the corporate culture.

INDUSTRIAL AGE

The birth of Scientific Management Theory.

THE TIMELINE OF WORK ATTITUDES

©2001 Catalyst Consulting Group, Inc.

work co-existed. During the agricultural age, for example, work songs helped turn dreary tasks and repetitive actions into activities that, if not fun, at least contained an element of anticipation and comfort. If they had to work, at least they could sing while they did it. Barn raisings were changed from a task impossible for one or two people into a picnic-style community event during which barns seemed to be born full-grown in a single day. The element of fun turned an impossible task into an anticipated one, one at which friends, family, and neighbors worked side by side for the common good, caught up on old times, and shared food with one another. Vestiges of this behavior can be seen today when groups of people get together on a Saturday to clean up a ball diamond, paint a senior citizen's house, or build a playground. Throughout history, there are many such examples of the integration of 'fun' with activities replete with the most boring and worst imaginable elements of work.

When the United States of America broke away from the Old World, Thomas Jefferson and the Founding Fathers put these words into The Declaration of Independence: "We hold these truths to be self-evident, that all men are created equal, that they are endowed by their Creator with certain unalienable Rights. That among these are Life, Liberty, and the pursuit of Happiness." During the last 150 years of industrial work behavior, the element of fun began to be isolated from work and treated as a discrete, separate, and segregated concept and activity. We had decreed fun to be separate from work. We had made fun at work taboo. Apparently, we no longer had the unalienable right to enjoy work while we pursued Happiness.

Today the concept of work is again in the midst of change. We are beginning to rediscover that fun belongs with work. It is my premise that fun and work naturally go together. That fun works and that work pays off better when it is fun. That for us to go forward, we need to unlearn 150 years worth of taboos about fun and work.

> "Love and work are the cornerstones of our humanness."
>
> SIGMUND FREUD

The integration of fun and work isn't about *what* you do, it's about *who* you're being when you're doing your work. Fun isn't the prize — it's the work. The enjoyment that comes with Cracker Jack® isn't simply the prize. The fun of Cracker Jack® is the process of finding the prize while you're eating the caramel corn and peanuts. If the fun were *only* the prize, that's all that would be in the box! But it isn't. Without the process, without the work, the prize would be meaningless. Enjoyment is a result of the integration of fun and work, of the Fun/Work Fusion.

When fun is integrated *with* work instead of segmented *from* work, the resultant fusion creates energy; it cements relationships between co-workers and between workers and the company. When fun is integrated *into* work, it fosters creativity and results in improved performance.

Over the years, companies have worked hard at improving things like their customer service and at improving their quality. Many dozens, if not hundreds, of books have been written and published on these two very important elements of successful business. What has been overlooked is the inestimable value of fun in work.

IN MY EFFORTS TO UNDERSTAND THE importance of the Fun/Work Fusion, I have formulated eleven principles for integrating fun and work. Principles which, if applied to your work, to your work relationships and to your company or business, will unleash creativity, foster good morale, and promote individual effectiveness.

In the creation of *Fun Works,* we researched companies whose behavior, attitudes, and systems illustrate the validity of these principles and also support the integration of fun and work with regard to each principle. Although I found dozens of companies who qualified, I chose to feature the ones that best represented each of the eleven specific Principles of Fun/Work Fusion. I spent months traveling to each company, interviewing key staff members, walking the facility, and witnessing the company at work. I took pictures and gathered collateral material. And I observed how each company embodied the principles of fun at work and determined which one they illustrated best. Their stories are located in Part Two: The Principles of Fun/Work Fusion.

Following are those principles, a brief explanation of each one, and a description of how that principle is represented by its case company.

PRINCIPLE ONE: GIVE PERMISSION TO PERFORM

Allow individuals to bring the best of their whole self to work each day. This principle requires a superb leader if it is to be effective. Leadership is essential to organizational well being. The leader creates the vision; the leader sets the tone for the journey; the leader holds the value that only by integrating fun and work can the best results be achieved. John Yokoyama, owner of Pike Place Fish in Seattle, Washington, World Famous home of the flying fish, believes play is the most important tenet. Employees interact with customers using play; they toss fish, they tell jokes, they dance with the customers. And when the play is done, Pike Place Fish has created employees who visit the fish market on their day off and customers who have committed to being customers for life.

PRINCIPLE TWO: CHALLENGE YOUR BIAS

Remove self-imposed obstacles to the release of your full being. We spend more time at work than any other single place, yet our biases prevent us from enjoying that time to its fullest. Our belief that 'when the work is done we can have some fun' may be the strongest obstacle we face to integrating fun in the workplace. Harvard University Dining Services (HUDS) actively encourages its employees to enjoy their work, to interact with Harvard students, and to think beyond the box. When new systems threatened old habits and comfort levels, HUDS encouraged its employees to consider the students first and do what was best for them — not necessarily what was best for themselves.

PRINCIPLE THREE: CAPITALIZE ON THE SPONTANEOUS

This is not a program but a philosophy. Fun doesn't necessarily happen on schedule; it grows in a culture that fosters its existence. Southwest Airlines (known for irreverent flight attendants, unassigned seats, and low fares) is a culture in which fun grows easily and quickly. And it generates profits, as well. The Southwest Philosophy is to hire nice people and create a working environment that is fun. They succeed.

PRINCIPLE FOUR: TRUST THE PROCESS

You can't muscle energy. A laugh that is forced is not a true laugh. Americans are experts at task orientation: we thrive on to-do lists. We need help, however, with process orientation: we need to trust our people and trust the process and then stand out of the way. Employease is an Internet Business Application Service Provider that offers web-based Human Resource services to a wide variety of companies. Their philosophy is: 'Successful management requires a lack of ego. Surround yourself with good people because it has a snowball effect. Good people give off more energy than they consume.' Employease has created a process that its employees love and follow with outstanding results.

PRINCIPLE FIVE: VALUE A DIVERSITY OF FUN STYLES

We don't all do it the same way. There is no right or wrong way to engage in serious fun. Be inclusive and share your fun energy with all constituents inside and outside of your organization. Blackboard, Inc., is a Washington DC based provider of Internet access for schools and their students, a place where both assignments and grades are posted for individual access by each student and each instructor. The wide variety of employees at Blackboard, Inc. has given rise to a wide variety of expressions of fun. Their philosophy is that work is hard but it's fun; that fun should exist before, during, and after work; that if work weren't fun, they wouldn't be doing it.

PRINCIPLE SIX: EXPAND THE BOUNDARIES

Don't start making rules to limit the process. The ideal balance of fun and work is only achieved when all individuals involved understand the boundaries of the playing field. At Process Creative Studios, an architectural firm in Cleveland, Ohio, the boundaries they have established along with the boundaries they have eliminated allow them to create award-winning designs, play a customer's original-music blues CD as their telephone on-hold music, and incorporate three large dogs into their daily in-office work lives.

PRINCIPLE SEVEN: BE AUTHENTIC

Where do you begin? All that is required is willingness: if you want to share this part of yourself with others, the opportunity will arise. To truly understand how work and fun integrate is to accept that it is a 'being' state, not a 'doing' state. Isle of Capri Casinos, Inc., one of the darlings of Wall Street, is a gaming industry leader in preferred-customer-marketing. Their 'Isle Style' attitude is not a veneer that's applied to a new employee, it's an internal quality that's naturally exhibited. Isle of Capri searches out authentic people who enjoy life and enjoy being around people, and then trains them in specific job skills *after* they've been hired.

PRINCIPLE EIGHT: BE CHOICEFUL

Embrace the whole person. To be choiceful means to give *yourself* permission. True fun is not something you choose to do, it is something you choose to be. Fun is deciding to bring the best of your whole self to work every day. Russell-Rogat was a Cleveland-based outplacement firm that valued 'Family First' and 'If it isn't fun we're out of here.' Success with the outplacement for the Panama Canal attracted the attention of Lee Hecht Harrison, a national outplacement firm highly respected in the industry. Because their cultures and values matched, they chose to merge. Their choices were appropriately rewarded.

PRINCIPLE NINE: HIRE GOOD PEOPLE AND GET OUT OF THEIR WAY

If you trust your employees with your organization's most valuable assets, why not trust them to use their judgment on bringing fun to their work? When the fun is 'in' the work and results from the satisfaction of good work and working relationships, then there is little risk of 'when the cat's away the mice will play.' One Prudential Exchange, a team of Prudential employees charged with the creation of a new culture for the insurance giant, was successful because Prudential hired for the team people who had passion for their work, confidence in their abilities, and the willingness to be vulnerable. And then they created an environment in which these people felt safe to say what was on their mind and lead the company to the achievement of their goals.

PRINCIPLE TEN: EMBRACE EXPANSIVE THINKING AND RISK TAKING

A culture that learns how to harness and develop the full potential of its employees is a culture that is comfortable with risk taking and expansive thinking. To be successful at risk taking, we must overcome our fear of failure. Will Vinton Studios, creator of the California Raisins and the M&M's commercials, believes in '...the value of taking risks and having fun while you do it. . . What we learn isn't as important as the learning itself. The most important thing we can learn is *how* to learn. . .risk taking for a company is essential. If you don't risk, you don't grow.' They live by their beliefs and their success is the yardstick by which these beliefs are judged.

PRINCIPLE ELEVEN: CELEBRATE

There is nothing more fun than the celebration of a success or a shared win. The celebration itself creates energy for ongoing efforts. What gets recognized gets repeated; what gets celebrated becomes a habit. Individual recognition and group celebration fuel high performance. American Skandia, a manufacturer and wholesaler of insurance and financial planning products and services to brokers and financial planners, takes great pains to make the effort to catch and compliment people doing something right. Like many of the successful companies featured in *Fun Works,* American Skandia hires for attitude and trains for skills. And they celebrate every success they can find.

IN ADDITION TO BEING ILLUSTRATED BY A CASE COMPANY, each of the Principles of Fun/Work Fusion has a key which, if turned by the reader, will help to unlock the principle so that it can be applied individually and/or to a company action plan. These keys are thoughts, actions, and behaviors that, if applied, will increase your ability to employ the specific principle in your life.

Because we human beings love to know how we rank in categories ranging from 'How good is your sex life?' to 'Do you know the three secrets to overnight financial success?', we have included in Part Four your own personal ranking test: The Fun/Work Fusion Inventory. This questionnaire should give you an indication of how much fun you are having at work and help you identify areas in which you can improve. Several action steps are suggested to help you get started in the full integration of fun and work.

Part Four also contains additional inspiration for you to use as you journey along the path of integrating fun and work.

FUN WORKS **IS INTENDED** to provide you with examples of companies who have successfully achieved the integration of fun and work in the hope that you, too, will discover the value of this natural condition and choose to create and live it for yourself.

We hope the process is as much fun for you as it was for us.

■

PART TWO
The Fun/Work Fusion Principles

"It is never too late to have
a happy childhood."

SCANDINAVIAN SAYING

1

PRINCIPLE ONE
Give Permission to Perform

ALLOW PEOPLE TO BRING THEIR WHOLE SELVES TO WORK EACH DAY

The concept of work is not static, it is fluid. As the world changes, so do our attitudes toward work. We are currently at a crossroads, at the creation of yet another attitude toward work. The new economy requires that we rethink what work is and what work should be. If work is going to attract the best people today and retain them tomorrow, then in addition to providing the resources to live, work must also be fulfilling.

People are demanding more from their jobs than merely a paycheck. They expect to enjoy what they do and they will search and move until they are satisfied with their work experience.

The shift to this new attitude toward work is not complete. We are still in the throes of breaking the bonds of traditional hierarchy in which employees won't take action without first getting permission.

- 'No one told me to do that.'
- 'It's not my job.'
- 'Do you have permission to do that?'

These are symptomatic phrases of our current status. If work is to be truly fulfilling for the worker, then our attitudes toward it will have to change. We will have to learn to trust ourselves and our co-workers to follow agreed upon guidelines rather than to consult the hierarchy before taking any action.

Instead of rules, restrictions, and limitations, we need Permission to Perform. Permission to Perform should include requirements for success, parameters of behavior and operation, and the permission to fail as well as the expectation to succeed. Permission to Perform is nothing more than empowerment as seen through the eyes of an entrepreneur. Entrepreneurs often don't have a hierarchy to consult. In fact, entrepreneurs often start their new businesses as an escape *from* someone else's hierarchy. Since they must get things done without the resources of a traditional hierarchy, entrepreneurs often hire independent contractors and/or outsource their work using only the conditions of Permission to Perform:

- 'Here's what I want and when I want it.'
- 'Don't spend more than this. Now, do it.'

- 'I don't need to hear from you until you're done.'
- 'You're the expert — that's why I hired you to do the work.'

Permission to Perform reduces the control of negative hierarchical guidelines and increases the opportunity for success of the worker. Historically, negative hierarchical guidelines for work outnumber and outrank the positive ones. We know what we can't do, what will get us in trouble, what not to say to whom, how far we can stretch deadlines, and how close to the line we can stand before we feel the wrath of the boss. What we don't know is how much of our selves we can and should bring to the job every day. Permission to Perform allows us to bring our whole selves to work each day. Bringing our whole selves means that fun and work must once again be integrated; the two can no longer be held apart.

Somewhere, sometime, some leader told us that work should not be fun; that work and fun cannot successfully coexist if a company is to be profitable; that fun at work is taboo. Since then, we have behaved as if fun cannot be part of our work experience. The companies profiled in *Fun Works* have shown, however, that fun and work can coexist, and do it both successfully and profitably. And, they have shown us that this coexistence is what workers want. The coexistence of fun and work is the emerging belief system on The Timeline of Work Attitudes.

To successfully transition to this new attitude toward work will take leaders who understand that fun and work *can* successfully and profitably coexist, that today's worker demands this integration; leaders who wholeheartedly and enthusiastically give Permission to Perform. It took leaders to create our current taboo against fun at work; it will take leaders to break that taboo and replace it with a new attitude. We need to become those leaders. We can no longer wait for permission, we must assume it; we can no longer wait for our employees to ask our permission, we must make them understand they already have it. That they have Permission to Perform.

There is no risk or downside in the long run to giving permission; the only risk we take is in withholding it. To succeed in business, give Permission to Perform and stand out of the way. Encourage employees to bring their whole selves to their work each and every day and everyone will reap the rewards.

■

World Famous
Pike Place Fish

The closest I've come to seeing a flying fish was in the early morning twilight in Seattle. I had seen the signs when I entered that read, "Caution, low flying fish," but I wasn't really prepared to see a 12-pound King Salmon fly through the air accompanied by a chorus of cries that said, "Pieces and fillets for Cleveland." And what was a new experience for me, throwing fish and yelling instructions like a Greek Chorus, is standard operating procedure for the Fun Works living laboratory of Give Permission to Perform, Pike Place Fish.

Shopping at Pike Place Fish, located in the Public Market in Seattle, Washington, is an event everyone should experience once in their lives; applying Pike Place Fish's philosophy to business and life is a strategy that can be employed by anyone who wants to become world famous!

When you get close to Pike Place Fish, you know something's different, that this is going to be an experience. Your first clue is a three-deep, half-circle of people standing around stainless steel carts loaded with whole fish, cooked crabs, clams, and other seafood delights, covered in layers of crushed ice. Then you notice that each face wears a smile and that they are laughing and giggling and poking each other. When you realize that many of them are taking money out of their purses and wallets, your first impression is that there must be a street performer in front of the chilled mackerel. In a way, you're right; the employees of Pike Place Fish are performing for their customers. They are working the crowd, making them happy, and priming them to buy fish. Lots of fish, I might add. I never thought that working in a fish market could be as much fun as these folks seemed to be having.

The avowed goal of Pike Place Fish is to be 'World Famous.' Pike Place Fish is one of three fish markets located on the Public Market Dock on Puget Sound in Downtown Seattle.

"We hold these truths to be self evident, that all men are

What makes Pike Place World Famous is a philosophy that integrates fun into their work, and lots of hard work means lots of fun. When John Yokoyama bought out the previous owner in 1965 for the sum of $3,500, Pike Place Fish was merely a fishmarket, unremarkable in many ways. It was a business that survived because of hard work, tough pricing, and keeping customers honest. In short, Yokoyama says, it wasn't a lot of fun. "Everyone here hated their jobs. I can remember the owner counting out loud the number of steps it took him to get a dozen clams for a customer and then complaining about it. So, when I took over, I operated the business the same way. We behave in ways we see others behaving. I was no different.

"For a long time, no one working here had fun. I was an angry manager; I was an angry

owner. The days were long and the work was hard. All the tools in my managerial tool kit were fear-based." Everyone had 'rules' to follow that were based on nothing more than 'how we've always done it here.' And no one had the permission to perform.

The change at Pike Place Fish started about ten years ago when the owner, managers, and employees decided they wanted to be world famous. And do it without spending a dime! The impetus for that change came after John attended an EST training session and followed that up with The Forum. "I let go. I decided that I didn't have to do it all. I let go of my ego. I realized that instead of demanding that the employees do things my way at my rate, I would empower them if I shared my vision." By sharing his vision with the staff, John had given them the permission to perform. They now had the opportunity to bring the best of themselves to their work every day. Nothing was holding them back. No longer was it acceptable to treat work as, well, work. If Pike Place Fish was going to be world famous, then work was going to have to be fun. And they had the permission to make it that!

"If we wanted to be world famous," John recalls, "then we had to decide to do it and act the way world famous fishmongers would act." John transformed from a yelling whip-cracker to the Fish King. His job now is to check the mood and make sure the energy is present. And to see to it that everyone on staff takes full advantage of their permission to perform.

Once Pike Place Fish came to their collective understanding, employee and owner attitudes and performances improved. And so did business. With these improvements came the creation of a Pike Place Fish style that was responsible for generating a new level of awareness.

created equal, that they are endowed by their Creator

After years of struggle and improvement, Pike Place Fish found itself in the apparent position of being an 'overnight success.'

This success drew the attention of various media including Chart House International's John Christensen who created one of the top selling documentary videos in the United States, *Fish*. In that video, Yokoyama described for the first time the Pike Place Fish Philosophy: Play; Make Their Day; Be There; Choose Your Attitude.

One of the interesting things about the Pike Place Fish style is that it is clearly visible. The first thing I noticed, for example, when I visited Pike Place Fish was the play. In order to interact better with the customers, and in order to make play easier, sales people stand *in front* of the stand with the iced fish *behind* them. This allows the employees to interact more directly with the clients. That interaction takes the expected form of talking and the unexpected forms of hugging, joke telling, praising, and fish throwing. When a customer decides on their purchase, a sales person, like Justin, will pick up the product, like a 12-pound King Salmon, and throw it over the rack of iced fish and the counter, some 10 to 15 feet, to someone like Bear, who will catch the fish, weigh it, wrap it, and collect the money. The flying fish toss, which looks like something out of Monty Python's Flying Circus, is accompanied by the yelled instructions from the sales person — "Pieces and fillets for Cleveland." Immediately, everyone behind the counter echoes "Pieces and fillets for Cleveland" in a chorus. This sort of behavior goes on constantly to the absolute delight of the customers and the throngs who have gathered to watch and experience Pike Place Fish.

We all know that Marketing 101 says that word of mouth is the best advertising. What Marketing 101 doesn't tell us is how to create word of mouth. "We deal in service to people," Jim B. says. "We give them the product they want but we also give them a show. We see people walk in here and they're stressed. We say hello and make them smile and they watch us having a good time. When they leave, whether they buy a fish or not, they're in a better mood. We've changed their attitude. We've made their day. And they tell people and maybe the next time they're in they buy a fish. At lunchtime, the younger business crowd comes in with their cartons of yogurt and watches us interact with the people. We call them the Yogurt Dudes. And when they go back to their sterile offices, they take something of us with them. We helped make their day."

with certain unalienable Rights, that among these are Life,

It's interesting to note that Pike Place Fish employees focus on making their customer's day, not on making the employees' day. When the focus is no longer on you but on your customers, play happens. Having fun is much easier to do when you get the focus off of you and onto those around you!

Every member of the Pike Place Fish team is aware of what's going on around them all the time, of who's saying what, of what a customer is saying or even what they're *not* saying! When you ask an employee a question, you can tell that they're actually listening to you. Even if the question you're asking is one they hear and answer 20 times a day. Their goal is to be there for you because when it's time to buy fish, they want to be there, too!

Along with the opportunity to be themselves that permission to perform gives the employees of Pike Place Fish comes a responsibility — the responsibility to choose their attitude.

Selling fish is a long and tiring job. Pike Place employees begin at 6:30 in morning and wind up their day at 6:30 in the evening. Most employees work the entire 12-hour shift. In order to achieve their goal of being world famous, employees are encourage to choose their attitude. "It's a long day," says Justin, "and it could be boring and tiring. Or I can choose to have fun. It's really that simple. It's up to me. I have the permission to perform and the ability to choose my attitude. When I choose to have fun, the time goes faster and I enjoy myself more. I don't want to get up at quarter to six each morning, but I do. And I decide to be happy. It's a simple choice and I make it." That choice makes it easier to be there for the customers, make their day, and turn a hard job into play.

But all this success doesn't just happen. It takes concerted effort. Pike Place Fish keeps on top of things with coaching; Jim B. is the business coach. "Everyone has the permission to coach anyone on staff. The lowest entry-level employee is allowed and encouraged to coach anyone, including John." Sammy, the assistant manager, explained the coaching as, "You're not telling them to make them wrong, you're telling them to make it right. It's up to them to decide to listen and make the necessary changes."

The staff of Pike Place Fish works on their development and relationships at bi-weekly meetings held in a casual setting over dinner. It's their goal to reconnect every two weeks with their intentions, including their intention to become world famous. The conversation, unlike the banter that takes place with their customers, is quite deep. Because they have permission to perform, individuals freely bring up their desires, their thoughts, their ideas, and readily acknowledge their responsibility to make Pike Place Fish world famous. Because they feel ownership, they provide constant input. When there is a breakdown between employees, they assume the responsibility to 'recreate the relationship' in order to have a breakthrough.

Liberty, and the pursuit of Happiness."

"When you make a stand for your vision," Jim explains, "the actions required for you to achieve that vision just seem to follow. Even breakdowns between employees or in our systems are not necessarily negative. Every break*down* has the ability to become a break*through* if you have the right attitude and talk about it."

The changes at Pike Place Fish can be traced to John Yokoyama's decision to let go, to give permission to each and every employee to perform by bringing their whole selves to their job; by giving them permission to have fun with their job. The shift to giving permission to perform has impacted Pike Place Fish in external ways which the customers see and feel every day, and also in  internal ways — the business is now valued at 1000 times more than John's original purchase price some 35 years ago. Pike Place Fish transacts more business per square foot during the Christmas season than any competitive grocery chain in the area. The business has expanded successfully into e-commerce, speaking engagements, training, and consulting. They have been the background for numerous films, television commercials, NBA announcements, and print ads. In addition, Pike Place Fish has been featured in two more Chart House International videos: *Fish Sticks,* and *Fish Tales.*

The vision of Pike Place Fish has also expanded. "We are not just fishmongers any more," explains John. "People buy here because of the relationships we create. Now we want to share the power of positive work relationships throughout the world. We want to promote world peace through goodwill."

Pike Place Fish is a Fun Works living laboratory of how Give Permission to Perform can change the lives of everyone it touches, improve the quality of life in the world and, in the process, make you world famous.

Without spending a dime!

■

THE DECLARATION OF INDEPENDENCE, JULY 4, 1776

Update: 2006

How does one measure success?

Terry Malloy, Marlon Brando's character in "On the Water Front" would have been happy to have been a heavyweight boxing contender, pleased to be remembered as being better than most but not quite good enough to be champion. In Terry's mind, the reason he never quite made it was not a failing on his part but was due instead to things beyond his control; things that conspired to keep him from achieving his dreams.

When the members of Pike Place Fish did their dreaming, they decided they wanted to be world famous. Once they reached that decision, they didn't wait for anyone to crown them champ. They simply assumed the throne by calling themselves World Famous. And then they acted World Famously. The secret to Pike Place Fish' success was that they gave themselves permission to be world famous; they moved from *doing* things that might make them money to *being* world famous. Once the cores of their beings were aligned with World Famous, world fame found them. It's perhaps the ultimate example of self-fulfilling prophecy.

At least once a year since I first interviewed John Yokoyama and the fishmongers of Pike Place Fish six years ago, I find myself in Seattle. Sometimes it's to visit friends, sometimes to do consulting, and several times to work on another book of mine, *Beans: Four Principles for Running a Business in Good Times or Bad* (a story about a successful coffee shop located four blocks up the hill from the Seattle Market that Pike Place Fish calls home).

Even when my trip to Seattle is tightly scheduled, I find the time to get down to Pike Place Fish. My routine is to anonymously slide into the back row of the crowd of customers waiting eagerly to

> *"The biggest mistake we could ever make in our lives is to think we work for anybody but ourselves."*
>
> BRIAN TRACY

spend their money on great fish and enjoy the good times. Each visit, I watch with joy the tossing of fish, the Greek chorus of "pieces and fillets," and the earnest and open conversations the fishmongers initiate with their customers, first-timers and regulars alike. And I smile at the smiles I see on the faces of fish purchasers, happy from the experience and glad to have been even a small part of Pike Place Fish' continuing story of success.

I stop by each time I'm in town to check up on that 'continuing story of success'. Too often when companies receive the adulation and world fame that has come the way of Pike Place Fish, it changes their nature and their culture and they crumble and fall apart. Under the thorny crown of fame, companies and individuals can lose themselves and everything they've worked for. Thirty years of toiling to become an overnight success can disappear quickly, the proverbial flash in the pan.

If I have concerns that Pike Place Fish might fall victim to the downside of being World Famous, they are quickly dispelled when Jaison or Bear looks up from the relationship he's just created with a customer, spots me, and waves, calling out a hearty 'hello.'

Soon we're standing off to the side, engaged in deep conversation. When I eventually walk away, in addition to purchased pounds of salmon and crab, I take with me a sense of comfort and peace that comes from having shared deep conversation with a fellow human being.

It was the practice of deep conversation that took John Yokoyama's nearly bankrupt fish business from the edge of disaster to the height of success. Twice a month, for nearly ten years, the staff of Pike Place Fish has gathered for dinner and deep conversation centered on who they wanted to become, who they wanted to be. The key to the success of those conversations was that they gave each other and themselves permission to perform. No one trampled on another's ideas, thoughts, or plans. Everyone allowed themselves to dream, to reach for the moon. From those conversations came the dream to be World Famous. These conversations also developed the concept of "It's over here" which says you have ultimate authority and power over who you are and who you want to become and no one else does. You decide to be happy, you decide to get up, and you decide to become a contender or even be World Famous.

As Pike Place Fish achieved its goal of being World Famous, it used these deep conversation dinners to envision its new future: World Peace, An Idea Whose Time Has Come.

John says to achieve this goal, just like they achieved their first goal, each member of the team has to be world peace. "We can't do this as a group. Groups don't accomplish things. Only members of groups acting and thinking individually can accomplish goals. It's up to each of us to be the things we want to achieve."

Pike Place Fish's success can also be measured in many standard ways. Dun & Bradstreet statistics show sales in 2005 of nearly $5,000,000. In addition to selling from their single location in the Seattle Market, shoppers can order fresh and frozen fish and seafood products from the web and have them delivered overnight packed in World Famous boxes and dry ice.

Pike Place Fish stories have appeared in a dozen books, twice as many magazines, and four times as many newspapers. They have been on television, on the radio, and in the movies.

John Yokoyama and the fishmongers ('the boys') have each written books that detail their success and lay out how the reader can achieve similar results. Four videos have been produced and sold worldwide by outside companies not affiliated with Pike Place Fish. And John and The Boys now give public speeches and seminars on how to run a business the Pike Place Fish way.

This, to me, is the ultimate measure of success: other people use *your* model to improve *their* lives. Clearly, the Pike Place Fish model has given others permission to unleash their fun selves.

To exemplify the P*lay* portion of the Fish philosophy, Kent State University's Communication and Marketing division has created "Pete The Perch," a stuffed animal that is awarded

monthly to a "deserving, hardworking, pleasant UCM staffer." Recipients come from nominations submitted by colleagues, clients, or members of the university community. UCM's *Be There* team created the Guppy Award for a student employee who "exemplifies the qualities and principles established by the FISH! Philosophy." The *Make Their Day* team has the Catch of the Month Award for teams or persons contributing to marketing projects.

When the president of First Essex Bank of Lawrence, Massachusetts decided that the bank would benefit from what the folks at Pike Place Fish had developed, he realized a top-down approach would most likely re-sult in just another 'management idea' reaction. To avoid this, the bank's trainer held a contest to determine which em-ployees had the best sense of humor. The winners in each department became the cadre that helped implement the Pike Place Fish concepts throughout the sys-tem. Eventually, the majority of employ-ees gave themselves Permission to Per-form and soon the solid First Essex Bank was experiencing Fun/Work Fusion.

Consumer Impact Marketing (a Canadian outsourcing firm focused on events, promotions, sales, and merchan-dising management) has fun as an ex-plicit part of its mission statement. By using the techniques developed by Pike Place Fish, their staff has improved its ability to add fun to their work, ensuring that clients and staff receive greater joy from their work.

Other notable companies who are finding the same sort of results include Thomas Cook Travel Agency, Community Bank of St. Louis, Tower City Title Agency in Cleveland, The Universalist Church of West Hartford, CT, and the Golden Colorado Police and Fire Dis-patch Center. (Their success in applying the Pike Place Fish principles was so effective that they were given an award by the National Emergency Number Association for "Outstanding performance as a team in providing professional emergency communications to the citizens of Golden." The $100 cash prize that went with the award purchased a fish tank into which each dispatcher has placed at least one fish as a reminder of their commitment to the team.)

Because John Yokoyama gave himself Permission to Perform, he created an environ-ment in which his employees felt comfortable to give themselves and each other Permission to Perform. Through its books and seminars, Pike Place Fish is reaching out and giving anyone who's interested Permission to Perform, encouraging others not to do exactly what Pike Place Fish does, but to be themselves in their own way. To *be* what inspires them and to commit to *being* who they say they are.

Many are those who are catching the fish being tossed their way by the folks at the Fun Works living laboratory of Give Permission to Perform, Pike Place Fish.

■

"The human race has only one effective weapon — and that is laughter."

MARK TWAIN

The Doing vs Being Key

THE 'DOING' STATE IS REINFORCED by American culture. We admire doers; we proudly admit to our Type A Behavior of 'get it done *now!*' Performance appraisals recognize the 'doingness' of our work contributions but they fail to ask the question: "What were you 'being' while you were getting the job done?"

Before we can successfully give or receive permission to perform, we must choose to experience our lives fully; we must learn to 'be' not just to 'do.' Before we can successfully integrate fun into our work, we must shift from a 'doing' state to a 'being' state.

To 'do' something fun is momentary; to 'be' fun is forever. 'Doing' feels like something that is outside of you — something that can be checked off a list. 'Being' comes from the inside — it is a deep reservoir that fills you up and is released like a breath, to be felt again with your next breath.

The two can coexist. The integration of fun and work is actually achieved when you are 'doing' *while* you are 'being.' The 'being' state is a connection to our inner core of thoughts, beliefs, feelings, and values. 'Being' is the true driver of 'doing.' It is far too easy, however, to become disconnected from 'being' under the pressure of time, focusing only on 'getting it done.' When you find yourself simply 'doing,' breathe some 'being' back into your life; bring some of your fun self to the project at hand. How do you 'be' fun? You choose it. 'Being' is a choice.

'Doing' your life is tiring; 'being' your life is revitalizing. 'Doing' takes energy; 'being' creates it. Imagine how effective we would be if we chose to shift from a culture that says 'Just Do It' to a culture that says 'Just Be It.'

To successfully receive or give permission to perform, choose to 'be.'

■

"Stress is the enemy.
It reduces your capacity
for engaging your fun self."

LESLIE YERKES

2

PRINCIPLE TWO
Challenge Your Bias

REMOVE SELF-IMPOSED BELIEFS
THAT ROADBLOCK THE RELEASE OF YOUR FULL BEING

We live with biases imbedded into our work ethic, biases that prevent us from integrating our whole selves into our work life. Do you carry with you any of these biases?

- 'If we have too much fun, then the work will not get done.'
- 'If I am silly, I may be perceived as stupid and/or unprofessional.'
- 'If I am fun-loving, it means I am less substantive.'
- 'It takes too much time to incorporate fun into the fabric of work.'
- 'Fun, joy, and passion are soft and have no relationship to effective work cultures.'
- 'Working hard and long are the prime requirements for creating and living a successful life.'

These biases are symptoms of our 'Type A Behavior.' We are fascinated with Type A; we glorify it and we honor it. We don't seem to value preparation and planning with anywhere near the amount of reverence we hold for 'rolling up our sleeves and getting right to work.' We value the result more than the method; we measure how much gets done instead of how much fun it was to do it. We often meet our deadlines but we don't grow and improve in the process.

When I give speeches, I always ask the audience what are the benefits of incorporating fun with work. The answers I get are always the same: a positive impact on morale and productivity; a reduction in stress, absenteeism, and attrition; and the ability to attract and retain key employees. Then I ask, 'If we understand that by incorporating fun into work we can achieve these results, what prevents us from doing that?' The answer I get is always our biases. And the chief among those is our bias that Type A Behavior is the desired norm.

We choose our biases; they are ours to keep or to let go. Why do we choose to keep the biases we have? For example, if we spend more time at work than at any other single activity, then why do we choose work that is sterile and bleak over work that is fun and enriching? The answer is fear.

We are afraid that if there is fun, there cannot be work; that if we are having fun, the outside world will think less of us. The companies in *Fun Works* have faced this fear and conquered it. They have incorporated the principle of challenging their biases and they have prospered. And in the process they have created a work environment that attracts and retains the kind of people who will further enrich these companies and increase their value.

The benefits of creating a work culture that places value on fun and productivity can be quantified. They can be measured in terms of employee satisfaction, retention, work quality, and customer loyalty. If your organization has strategic initiatives such as: *Finding and Keeping Peak Performers, Innovation in Products and Services, Quality and Service as a Competitive Advantage, Managing the Risks of Stress and Change, Increased Productivity,* and *Employee Satisfaction,* then the principle of Challenge Your Bias will help you achieve these initiatives more quickly.

When we challenge our bias of 'when the work is done then we'll have fun' and incorporate fun into work, then our self-imposed obstacles to success will be removed.

Take down those roadblocks that prevent the full release of your being. Change the way you think about the value of integrating fun and work. Challenge the status quo and take control of your attitudes toward work.

Challenge your bias.

■

"Remember that happiness
is a way of travel,
not a destination."

ROY GOODMAN

Harvard University
Dining Services

Driving through Boston and Cambridge on my way to Harvard University was an experience that produced an unusual sensation within me — I felt like I was traveling both back in time and into the future, simultaneously. Michael J. Fox had nothing on me!

Cambridge is alive with tradition, classic New England clapboard homes, and sidewalks made of cobblestones and bricks. And in the very center of town is Harvard University, America's oldest institution of learning, founded as a college in 1636. The physical campus of Harvard, replete with English-University-style buildings dating back to 1720, exudes tradition, history, and constancy. Yet the campus atmosphere (it was the first day of summer school) vibrates with freshness, vitality, and change. I knew that my journey to this Fun Works living laboratory of Challenge Your Bias, Harvard University Dining Services (HUDS), would be filled with great examples of thinking outside the box — of bias being challenged and overcome.

When you think of college food, you have a certain preconception, a certain bias, based both on personal experience and 'common knowledge' — college food is on a par with hospital food or airline food: it's not very good. Awful is also a word you'll hear in the same sentence with college food. Mystery meat comes to mind as well. It may surprise you to learn that when I was choosing a college, one of my criteria for where I would go was to choose a school that wasn't served by SAGA Food Services. Let me explain.

When I was young, my father was a food service manager for SAGA at Oberlin College, Case Western Reserve University, and The University of Akron. I grew up in college kitchens watching chefs cook and bake. I loved the experience and I thought the food was great. My reason for *not* choosing a SAGA-connected school was not the food, but that I knew I would find a part-time job working in food services and I didn't want it to be a direct line to my father!

I never thought much about college food after I graduated until I heard about HUDS from a colleague. I was impressed when I saw that Harvard University thinks so much of its food service program and food's role in the college experience, that it sends out a full-color brochure to new students explaining, in great loving detail, what it will be like to eat at Harvard during their four years of residency. If I had only known!

Harvard follows the English tradition of creating Houses for its students. Each year, some 2,000 freshman live in a series of dorms that surround all four sides of Harvard Yard. Freshmen eat with other freshmen in Annenberg Hall, a mammoth dining room that can seat over two thousand in a meal period. In their sophomore year, students are assigned to a House where they will live for the duration of their stay at Harvard. These Houses, accom-

modating between 350 and 450 students each, are complete with a kitchen and dining room and all meals are taken there. Harvard believes that community and social dialogue are aided and abetted by food. "The dining hall is where students at Harvard have their first discourse," explains Alexandra McNitt, Assistant Director for Marketing & Communications. "Food is key at Harvard. Over meals you have discourse which creates community. Food is necessary for life and so is discourse. The University feels very strongly that meals are part of the educational process." The University has taken great pains to see that these interactions occur, improving the college experience for all students. The question becomes, how do you make the food live up to the process? The answer is you challenge your bias and overcome it.

In the early 1990s, Mike Berry was brought in by the University to assume the directorship of HUDS. Berry was a charismatic man and a change agent. "Mike brought fun to food services," Alexandra remembers. "He was nuts. He took a formerly staid organization and created positive chaos. Working with Mike was a big roller coaster ride; he always made you feel like a million dollars. We did new things; we learned new ways. We made a lot of changes in how we thought and how we performed. Mike hired Michael Miller to become our Executive Chef in order to bring variety to the sameness of our food. Mike Berry helped us create massive changes at a time when we needed a top-to-bottom management approach. By the time Ted (Mayer, the current HUDS Director) came on board, we needed to shift to a more detail-oriented approach to change, and we needed to discover how to bring that approach closer to the needs and desires of our students."

Harvard University Dining Services is a huge operation. It employs more than 650 people in 26 units and supports 13 undergraduate houses (each serving up to 400 students three times a day), a dozen full-service restaurants open to the University community, their guests as well as students, and a full-service catering operation, Crimson Catering. During Commencement Week alone, HUDS caters 265 themed events providing 85,000 meals. In the course of an average year, they serve up more than 5,000,000 meals! HUDS has won numerous awards including the 1995 Visionary Award conferred by the Food Group and Creative Food Solutions, four

1996 Horton Awards, a 1996 Ivy Award conferred by *Restaurants & Institution Magazine*, two 1997 Horton Awards, two 1998 Horton Awards, and two 2000 Horton Awards. Internal recognition comes from no less than Harvard University Provost, Harvey Fineberg, who considers Harvard University Dining Services to be the benchmark of service for *all* the divisions of Harvard University! Each year the Harvard President confers the Harvard Heroes Award. Many individuals and teams from HUDS have been recognized for their contributions to the University.

Many of the changes that have been exhibited by HUDS, as well as many of the awards it has received, can be traced to August 1997, when Ted Mayer convened 58 managers and a dozen hourly employees, representing a cross-section of jobs and responsibilities, for a three-day retreat at Cranwell Resort in Massachusetts. The results of that meeting have become so monumental that the event is termed simply 'Cranwell' and has come to define the turning point in HUDS operations and execution of its strategic plan. From Cranwell came the imperative to change. Goals were outlined in a five-point plan: Create a new vision statement; Design a management development strategy and performance management system; Develop new production and delivery systems; Increase food quality; and Adopt new financial systems.

"It's kind of fun to
do the impossible."

WALT DISNEY

To ensure Cranwell's success, HUDS participated in the creation of a vision for its entire staff of 650 employees, a vision that would both excite them and include them. One of the first tangible results of that vision was the renovation of the kitchens in Eliot and Kirkland Houses.

Changing the kitchens in these two historic Houses created its share of skepticism and problems, of bias to overcome. The Masters of each House insisted that the overall tone of what was changed and/or added had to maintain the original architecture and home-like am-

biance that had existed for hundreds of years. Yet what was needed was a modern, *new* way of providing and serving food. The result was a combination of a self-serve scatter system (a sandwich making center, a cereal bar, a salad bar, and hot dinners served from the woks and pans in which they were created) and open kitchen areas where the chefs cook to order on grills, ranges, and woks right in front of the students. With much thought and compromise (overcoming bias), plans were created which satisfied both goals: a modern approach with a traditional look. The changes were enthusiastically supported by the House Masters and students alike and have been written up with lavish praise in publications such as: *The Crimson, Campus Dining Today, Nation's Restaurant News, Harvard University Gazette, The Harvard Independent, Food Management,* and *Seafood Leader* to name a few.

The staff, however, still had a few biases to overcome.

"This unit has experienced enormous change," says the Manager of The Culinary Support Group, Andy Allen. "We've had to almost totally throw away fifteen years of experience and disregard the way we've always done things. It's a new mindset and at first we had a lot of resistance. For example, with our new systems, we've improved and increased the size of our central cooking facility and minimized the cooking area in the Houses. In the past, the product sat around in the Houses constantly over heat and lost both visual appeal and flavor. Today, we have a technology called blast-chill. We partially cook foods, chill them immediately, and ship them in plastic bags to the Houses. The chefs at each House keep the bags refrigerated and pull them out in small units to heat, only when they need them. Once our people got over their feeling that the product wouldn't be as good (and the products are excellent), we're having a lot of fun inventing recipes and trying new items that we can blast-chill and put into the system. In order for these changes to happen, we had to get past our feelings that something wouldn't work.

"My job is to help our staff by getting them to discuss their feelings, to vent their frustrations, and then get them to come up with new ideas we can try. I have to take the time in the midst of change and the everyday chaos that's part of the food service environment and listen to them. My role is to make sure that this place stays on the right path. To build a family atmosphere, we greet each other every morning. Saying hello is very important. We take time to talk. Because we've achieved some success with Cranwell, we get a lot of visitors in our kitchen so we've all worked hard to clean up our language and humor, both of which are notoriously bad in kitchen environments!

"My job is to have the tools they need, make sure we get the work done, and have fun in the process. I do that by helping them think out of the box, supporting them, and letting them do their work by setting expectations and boundaries."

Andy is dynamic and forceful, a ball of energy. He is Yang to the low-key, patient, persistent, and detail-focused Yin of HUDS Director, Ted Mayer.

"I try to run Harvard University Dining Services as if it were a separate company contracting with Harvard University," Mayer says. "I think about cost, expense, service, attitude, and product. Instead of acting like we'll always be here, I run our department as if we could be replaced by a contractor who might do a better job. That helps us stay focused on our customer, the student. It's very important for us to have fun every day in our jobs because that fun shows and it helps to create a good relationship with the students, who are our very reason for being. Happy people are much more expansive and willing to share and willing to extend themselves to the customers. Plus, it's good business to think and act this way.

"It's hard, sometimes, to do that, to have fun all the time, because when we're working and are under stress, our customers are relaxing and enjoying themselves, three times a day, seven days a week. The two are at odds. We have to remember that we are part of someone else's positive experience.

"I try to keep in mind that we're not just in the food business, we're in the education business. We just deal with food and there's no better or more common currency. Our customers are here to learn, to experience, to grow. It's our job to help them do that. And do it in an enjoyable manner.

"I've discovered that our employees do better and have more fun when they're busy. And they do that best when they bring their whole selves to the experience. When they do, it's easier for them to balance work and fun. It's important for 'what you're doing' to be 'what you're being.'

"My vision for HUDS is to create the energy so people enjoy their work and then take ownership of it. Employees must have a passion for food and people and fun."

Bob Leandro, Assistant Director for Residential Dining has those passions but he has to admit that he's had to overcome some of his biases along the way. "We had a HUDS award ceremony one year and our management team decided to perform a parody of 'A Chorus Line' called 'A Serving Line.' I was willing to go along and be part of the group but I really didn't see what good it would do. My perception was that it wasn't such a good idea and wouldn't achieve anything positive. I guess, if left to my own devices, I wouldn't have done it. But I learned the words and the music and the steps and I did it. I was blown away by the response! The entire audience was on its feet from the beginning whistling and clapping and cheering. They were cheering so loudly that they couldn't really hear us but they were able to read the words and sing along from the slides that were projected overhead. But what was amazing was how they got into it. It was such a powerful experience that I'm getting goose bumps right now telling you about it. I learned that in every idea there's a little fear of failure. And that no matter how much I might not think something new will work, it's worth it to take a chance. 'A Serving Line' turned out to be fun. Our staff discovered that the

managers were more like them, more human, than they thought. I've never worked so hard at something and loved it so much!

"Another idea I didn't think was going to work was the Winnie-the-Pooh Tea. When someone first proposed it, I was certain these students were too sophisticated to become involved. But I was wrong! All kinds of kids came to the tea wearing their Winnie-the-Pooh shirts and pajamas, bringing books and Pooh Bears and all sorts of things. Originally, I thought the idea was whacked, but the students really enjoyed it.

"I'm a fun-loving guy but I guess I still have preconceptions about what will and won't work. I've learned that if I can get past my bias, I'll learn more and have more fun."

Executive Chef Michael Miller also has to admit to a little preconception and bias, too. "When we talked about holding a seniors-only cooking class, sort of a last-minute survival tips for the real world, I wasn't sure how many would sign up. We had so many interested that we had to create several more sessions just to get them all in!

"I meet with the students in each House at least twice a year and I try to eliminate any bias I might bring with me from years of doing food service. I have to remember to listen to the students as my customers and provide service. One time a student said he missed his favorite soft drink, Minute Maid orange soda. I knew we couldn't physically fit another flavor into our machines and the standard response would be to say, 'I'm sorry, we can't accommodate you.' But I decided he had the right to want his favorite soft drink so I had the staff order two cases of it and send it to his room. It cost us less than $10 and he was thrilled. That's the kind of out of the box thinking we have to remember to do to be successful. Plus, it makes you feel good when you can solve a problem like that.

"The HUDS staff works together to make each other look good. We don't tolerate any undermining and we have explicit expectations. And we always keep in mind that the student is our customer. It's our job to make their college experience a good one."

The success of the Harvard University Dining Services is a great example of how overcoming bias can make work fun, of how it can improve learning, and make the experience for the customer a joyful one. Mike Miller likes to tell this story that illustrates why his job is so much fun. "The most important and momentous occasion for any Harvard student is their graduation on Harvard Yard," Mike declares. "It's the culmination of four years of hard work and heart-warming friendship. It's a very personal moment, one that's shared with family and those friends who've experienced it along with the graduating senior. You can imagine how deeply touched I was, then, when last year two students with whom I'd become friends rushed over to me in their robes immediately following the ceremony to have their pictures taken with me! That says everything about the power of food and what we're doing here at Harvard."

That kind of meaningful result has become more and more common for Harvard University Dining Services as they overcome their bias and lead the entire University as the benchmark of good service.

If only food and food service had been as good as this when we were in school!

■

Update: 2006

W e're at our best when we have an emergency," says Rudolf Gautschi, Director for Residential Dining. And I believe him because on this May morning in Boston, it's been raining for three days, roads are closed, employees are having difficulty getting to work, the tunnels between the kitchens and the Houses (student dormitories) have flowing water in them, and yet our breakfast meeting is going off without a hitch. Other than staying dry on the walk over, my only problem has been deciding what I'd like the chef at Mather House to make me for breakfast.

Since I last visited Harvard University Dining Services in Boston, a lot has changed; and a lot hasn't. "It's always like that," says Executive Chef Larry Kessler, "the more things change, the more they stay the same." Harvard University, steeped in hundreds of years of tradition and housed in a wide-range of architecturally classic buildings, finds itself at the cutting edge of change in many areas, none more significant or impressive than that associated with HUDS. Since the arrival of Ted Mayer, Executive Director of HUDS, the country's oldest dining service has moved from one that used to serve institutional food reheated in steam table lines to one that receives kudos for the high-quality food it serves and for the positive community it creates and relationships it builds.

The program to change Harvard's dining experiences from standard to exceptional required physical changes to the facilities. Mather House is the last of thirteen facilities to be renovated and remodeled on the Harvard Campus—two years ahead of schedule, yet still under the projected $34,000,000 budget. During the same time, HUDS' revenues have increased to nearly $50,000,000 and the staff has grown to nearly 600 at 30 locations, which include residential, catering, and restaurant operations.

Since my last visit, HUDS' accomplishments have received the enthusiastic approval of many outside agencies. Mayer received the 2002 Leadership Award from *Food Management Magazine* and the 2006 International Foodservice Manufacturers Association Silver Plate Award, presented to the nation's top operator in the college and university market. In these same six years, HUDS collectively and individually received many other national awards (see partial list on page 41).

Awards are nice, Mayer says, but what he and his staff value the most is the reward they get from satisfied faculty and students who heartily approve of the meals and service they receive every day, seven days a week, from HUDS. "We deal with eighteen- to twenty-year-olds," says Crista Martin Assistant Director for Marketing. "We try not to take ourselves too seriously even though our work is serious. But so is theirs. Our job is to provide them with good food, good nutrition, and some relief from the stresses of the day." The

success of their efforts is documented by the results of the constant surveying they do. In those surveys, Harvard students give overwhelmingly positive marks to the quality, variety, and presentation of the food available in their Houses. But what's most telling is the nearly 95% approval students give to the quality of service provided by the HUDS staff, service that includes appearance, friendliness, and response to personal requests. College food has certainly come a long way from when I was in school.

Further proof of the power of HUDS' culture of fun at work, is that retention of staff at all levels remains high and that the newly hired are consistently the brightest and best available.

Rudy Gautschi, born and raised in Switzerland, has more than 25 years of food and beverage experience working for Hyatt and Marriott Hotels and as Director of Foodservice at Brigham & Woman's Hospital. He brought with him an outmoded management style, a bias he had to challenge. "Originally, everything I focused on and all my efforts were about productivity—how much could you get done in how little time by how few people. That was my management style. But once I got here, I discovered this style simply didn't work as effectively any longer. So now I do that MBWA thing—Management by Walking Around. I must spend 40% of my time walking between houses and kitchens. With a residential dinning team of 35 managers and 350 hourly employees, I have to be more than just a boss, telling them what do and when to do it. I have to be a leader and I have to interact with them in person." Like most of the folks at HUDS, Rudy Gautschi gets the big things right as well as the little things that make the big things work better. "By nature, I'm a fun guy. You have to have fun. If you can't, then something is seriously wrong. I discovered that when I use that part of me when I'm leading, I get better results. I used to be a master of all the hard science—how to do what when. Now, I'm learning to master the softer side, the little things.

And it's the combination of the two that really works. No matter how hard things get, or what kind of emergency we might have, when we're enjoying what we're doing, we're doing those things better."

Judith Della Barba, Director for Human Resources and a HUDS employee for nearly nine years, says "It's not about you, it's about the organization. It's about low ego and high pride." The height of pride for HUDS comes once a year—commencement. "During this most hectic, demanding and fulfilling time of the year," Judy says, "it's all hands on deck. There are no titles during commencement week, just worker bees getting done whatever needs to be done. It's the most physically and mentally exhausting work we do all year. But at the same time, it's the most fun and the most rewarding. In all ways, this is HUDS' commencement, too. It's the culmination of our year. It's our grand time on stage."

Their time on stage is not without financial rewards, either. One third of HUDS revenues are generated in this seven-day period. What is the scope of the physical requirements? In one week HUDS caters more than 80,000 individual meals. On Class Day alone, HUDS prepares 5,500 sandwiches (hand-slicing 4,000 Kaiser rolls and 5,500 tomatoes) and bakes more than 10,000 brownies. 19,000 chairs are set up, taken down, set up, wiped off, and taken down again. 36,000 bottles of water are consumed along with 9,600 bottles of beer, 2,400 bottles of wine, 64 cases of scotch, bourbon, gin, and rum. And while there are problems every year, every year they are conquered and Harvard graduates step into their future under the hospitality of HUDS.

As HUDS looks to its future, Mayer and his staff find themselves in the forefront of yet another cutting-edge program: FLP, the Food Literacy Project. Realizing that we are what we eat, but that most of us have no clue about what's in our food or what we *ought* to eat, HUDS started FLP to inform students of portion size, nutrition, and cause and effect of the things we put in our bodies. FLP focuses on purchasing locally grown and harvested products, providing ethnic foods, educating on the political nature of foods (fair trade items), and teaching how to cook for yourself. In fact, that original one-time-only, how-to-cook class started by HUDS several years ago has now become a two-week program for graduating seniors, many of whom claim they learn more useful things and discover more information from the food prep class than from any other course on campus.

Ted Mayer's job is to create good food, but his mission is to create good community. "We're proud of the Food Literacy Project. It's not only about helping people to eat healthy and wisely, it's about building community, about creating a feeling of being a partner with the students and not just a vendor serving them food. Because of all our various experiences and successes, HUDS brings an expertise in building community to the entire University. And we're as proud of that as we are of our food. Our staff feels the same way I do. We all have this great sense of adding value. We work hard. We allow our employees to express both sorrow and joy. We care about them as family. If you want people to be nurturing, you have to nurture them. That's how you build community and that's what our culture is all about."

Cultures that require their members to consistently challenge their bias expand new frontiers, generate new ideas, produce positive results, and successfully blend fun with work. HUDS, as documented by student surveys, peer recognition, employee satisfaction, and industry awards is such culture, which more than likely insures the continued success of Harvard University Dining Services.

HUDS AWARDS

- Eleven NACUFS prestigious Horton Awards

- *Food Management Magazine*
  1999 Best Concepts Award: Customer Service
  2002 Leadership Award
  2005 Best Concepts Award: Renovation

- 2005 Massachusetts Innovation and Technology Exchange Award for website design

- American Culinary Federation Team Competition
  2003 and 2004 First Place and Gold Medals

- University & College Designers Association, 2004 Silver Medal and Award for Excellence

"When I am flexible and forgiving, I am happy.
When I am rigid and righteous, I am unhappy.
It's that simple."

Hugh Prather, "Spiritual Notes to Myself"

The Forgiveness Key

ONE OF THE STRONGEST BIASES that blocks our potential to create fun-based relationships is the bias created by a grudge — our inability or unwillingness to forgive.

A grudge keeps a relationship from 'being;' it prevents synergy from happening. A grudge stands in the way of success like a lift bridge with the center section raised. If we are to bring our whole self to our work, if we are to 'be' fun, then we must lower that impassable section of the bridge and make it whole it again. We must let it go, get over it; we must forgive.

To bring your full, fun self to your work relationships, remove the layers of grudges and betrayals that insulate your heart. When your heart joins your head and hands in your work, you will have released one of the most powerful forces in your life — the energy of your whole being.

Our heart is like a computer hard drive — a large and expansive space, but one that can and does get filled up. What fills your heart? Is it filled with pain, fear, and grudges? Or have you discovered the cleansing power of forgiveness? Is your energy devoted to maintaining barriers and grudges, or is it targeted to creating possibilities?

Remove a powerful bias in your life, eliminate your grudges.

Forgive.

■

"Let us realize that the privilege to work is a gift, that power to work is a blessing, that love of work is success."

DAVID O. McKAY

PRINCIPLE THREE
Capitalize on the Spontaneous

THIS IS NOT A PROGRAM BUT A PHILOSOPHY.
IT'S NOT WHAT YOU DO, IT'S WHO YOU ARE

Fun doesn't happen according to schedule. It isn't something we plan. Fun grows in a culture that fosters its existence; it springs automatically from the proper environment. Don't inhibit its existence by scheduling too tightly; allow room for it to breathe and grow.

Fun will replicate itself if encouraged. It is naturally contagious and knows no hierarchical boundary. Fun will instinctively assume new forms and delight us with its unexpected changes and variations.

Capitalize on the spontaneous. Don't over think it, keep it simple.

∎

"Laughter is the sun
that drives winter
from the human face."

VICTOR HUGO

Southwest
Airlines

How do you take a cocktail-napkin idea and turn it into the most profitable airline in America? You utilize your warrior mentality to defeat your competition and rely on your ability to have spontaneous fun to enchant your customers. And when you're finished, what you have is Southwest Airlines — the most fun you can have flying for peanuts.

If you've flown a commercial airline in the last ten years, your flight has been affected in some manner by the success that Southwest Airlines has had in their thirty-year history. And if you've ever flown Southwest Airlines, you've been affected by the personality and charisma of their employees — something called SWA, the Southwest Attitude. Most likely, however, you're unaware of the business acumen and hard-nosed realities that were behind the creation of its fun-a-minute style.

In 1966, Rollin King, a somewhat unsuccessful commuter airline owner (he was losing money and trying to sell it off!) met with his lawyer, Herb Kelleher, to talk about his vision for the future — an airline that flew between Dallas, Houston, and San Antonio cheaper and faster than you could drive there by car. In what they recall as a very short meeting, Kelleher listened to King's ideas and replied, "Rollin, you're crazy. Let's do it."

And thus was born Southwest Airlines, America's fun-loving way to fly.

But before that could become a reality, however, Kelleher and King had to wrest every ounce of energy from their warrior mentalities, and more money than they had, just to get the freedom to legally exist. More than five years of court battles had to be won before the first flight of Southwest Airlines on June 18, 1971. During the years that followed, Southwest has been 'attacked' by the biggest

> **KEEP A WARRIOR SPIRIT**
> When it comes to dealing with the competition, Southwest employees mount a good offense. They have a history of aggressively going into battle. In fact, Southwest is half-assed about nothing! The company believes if you're going to do something, do it with intensity and do it right.
> Kevin & Jackie Freiberg
> *Nuts: Southwest Airlines' Crazy Recipe for Business and Personal Success*,
> p. 152

names in the airline industry. Each attack was engaged by Southwest and the battle won. Some of those victories have changed the face of flying. For example, in 1994 several major airlines led a movement that resulted in Southwest Airlines being blocked out of the Travel Reservation Network. This was an attempt to make it difficult for people to obtain tickets to travel on Southwest. Rather than go through a long and costly legal battle, on January 31, 1995, Southwest created and launched Ticketless Travel — a concept that has since become an industry standard.

Southwest has been rewarded in many ways for its independent spirit and indomitable will to succeed. In October 1996, the Department of Transportation's Air Travel Consumer Report rated Southwest as having the best ontime performance, best baggage handling, and fewest customer complaints for an unprecedented fifth consecutive year. SWA calls this the 'Triple Crown Award.' As of June 2000, Southwest ranked number one in fewest customer complaints for the last eight years and number one in ontime performance for the last seven.

> **FUN**
> **Employees are encouraged to take their jobs and the competition seriously — but not themselves. The company is serious about creating an environment where play, humor, creativity, and laughter flourish. Southwest believes that people having a good time are more stimulated and more themselves. Southwest rejects the idea that work has to be serious in order for people to accomplish great things.**
> **Kevin & Jackie Freiberg**
> *Nuts: Southwest Airlines' Crazy Recipe for Business and Personal Success*,
> p. 148

Awards like these are the result of Kelleher and King's commitment to make airline travel a fun experience, not an ordeal.

"Ladies and Gentlemen, the captain has turned on the Fasten Seat Belt sign. Please keep your hands and legs inside the plane at all times." When I first heard a Southwest flight attendant make that remark, I laughed out loud. As I did when I heard this one: "Flight attendants, prepare your hair for arrival." It's comments like these that continually make me smile and turn the often-boring rigors of travel into an experience not to be missed. When flight personnel are obviously having a good time, I find myself having a good time, too.

Finding the right people is a demanding, but fun process. In 1998, for example, Southwest received 141,710 résumés and hired only 4,115 new employees. Sandra Provost, Corporate Recruiter, says, "We hire the person, not the résumé. We're looking not only for people with a sense of humor but for someone who can be spontaneous. Things happen quickly and you've got to be able to come up with a quick response. Sometimes the response will have better results if it's humorous. Our people need to have good judgment and quick wits. When we're interviewing flight attendants, we no longer ask them *why* they want to work for Southwest because we know their answer will be that we're a fun place to work. What we ask them to do is to tell us about an incident in their life when they had to use humor in a situation, and what the result was. We want our new employees to understand that work should be fun; that it's okay to jump and scream and have fun at work.

"We also have behavior-based interviewing that gives us a good clue as to the kind of person they are. But often something spontaneous happens that gives us an even better idea. Once a pilot of ours sat in the waiting room and pretended to be applying for a flight attendant's job. Sometimes all the recruiters wear pajamas; sometimes we wear our clothes backwards. We watch the candidates to see how they respond to those kinds of things and what they do. If they are offended or put off, we know they wouldn't be right for Southwest. Our criteria are: fun, teamwork, communication, we versus I, common sense, decision making, flexibility, initiative, and being a self-starter. We hire nice people, then we create an environment that is fun."

Kelleher says, "We are looking for liberated, fun-loving people. We want you to be what you are, don't deny it. Be good at it! In our advertising, we promote our people as the best in the industry. That's a tremendous risk for anyone but in our case, our people *are* the best."

One of the first things I noticed inside their Dallas Headquarters was that, in keeping with Southwest's themes of creating a fun environment and keeping costs low, the walls do not contain 'corporate' art but are instead covered with photos of Southwest employees: employees having fun, at parties, in impromptu situations, and engaged in some of their many community services. The Hearts & Homes project saw Southwest's Dallas employees rejuvenating homes in poorer neighborhoods; in Operation Cover-Up, San Francisco's employees painted over graffiti on public walls and bridges.

Throughout the corporate structure of Southwest, teams that form, for fun and work, cut across hierarchical lines — pilots, ground crew, and office personnel intermingle on a first name basis. This sort of family approach is instrumental in creating and maintaining the sense of fun that you feel whenever you interact with Southwest Airlines. That family spirit makes the company strong in other ways, as well.

> "Laugh and the world laughs with you."

At one point, United Airlines attempted to compete with Southwest's low fares by launching United Airlines Shuttle Service. Although supported by a national effort and a completely funded budget, United's Shuttle Service failed because it failed to match Southwest's family spirit and dedication. Unwilling to let any of their competitors stay in business by charging less to fly, Southwest, supported by its employees, proved that low fares is not a gimmick to them; it's a way of life.

So is Spontaneous Fun.

Paul Quinn, retired Vice President of Schedule Planning, wanted to reward his staff for their superior service. His budget wasn't large enough to take them all out to dinner, so he brought in his grill and threw them a Texas barbecue. Needless to say Quinn's fete was a success. It was such a success, in fact, that it quickly turned into a regular Friday tradition. When Southwest constructed its new headquarters, a deck was built in back so Quinn's barbecue could continue. Today, even after Quinn's retirement, the deck parties serve thousands of people and are held every Friday when the weather's good.

The Chili Cook Off started out the same way — someone at one Southwest branch office decided to have a chili-cooking contest. The idea spread, and now it's in its 27th year and it's system-wide.

"We do develop traditions," says Libby Sartain, Vice President of The People's Department,  "but we try not to institutionalize them. If it's fun, it's fun. If it doesn't work in Tulsa, they don't do it. If you don't want to do it twice or do it the same way, you don't have to. Fun is spontaneous and that's how we like to be."

Each airport location is encouraged to operate its facility as if it were its own Southwest Airlines — subject to FAA regulations, the company mission statement, and certain obvious requirements. This autonomy further enhances the family feeling — individual units who are part of a larger, extended family. What works in Baltimore may not fly, so to speak, in Seattle.

Even though there are now 56 cities and 57 airports served by more than 29,000 Southwest Airlines employees, communication is important and frequent. Colleen Barrett, Executive Vice President of Customers, sends long and frequent memos that keep employees up to speed on what's happening. "While Southwest was actually cited by some members of Congress for being a 'good airline,'" a Colleen memo to all SWA employees from October 11, 1999 states, "it is very important that we not rest on our laurels. We each must assume personal responsibility and stand accountable for the contents of the Customer Service Commitment. Remember, the time to improve is when we are at the top of our game!" The memo continues with several pages of tips. Some of the highlights include:

- **Be flexible, use common sense and good judgment, and do the right thing regardless of our rules or procedures.**
- **Avoid using airline jargon.**
- **Share your own Customer Service Tips that have worked for you in the past with your fellow workers.**
- **Have fun with your fellow workers and with your customers.**
- **Look for ways to turn lemons into lemonade.**
- **Never say: 'It's against company policy.' Sometimes the right thing to do is to go against company policy.**

Company Policy at Southwest is actually quite small for such a large company. Common Sense and Use Your Own Judgment seem to replace the pages and pages of rules and regulations found in many American firms of the same size. Kelleher's attitude about what Southwest is, goes a long way to explain that. "This is not a company; this is a family where everyone is well-loved, well-respected, and well-thought-of," he says. "That's very important to each one of us personally."

Like families, companies have identities. In business it's called their culture. In order to see to it that Southwest's culture has a life of its own, Southwest University goes out to newly opening locations and sets up the ground rules and helps them create their own culture. Since every location is treated as a separate entity, a culture committee is started. This committee will decide for themselves what they will do and how they will do it. This sort of informal structure requires spontaneity if it is to exist. Spontaneous fun is a logical result, then, of a culture that values unstructured evaluation and response to stimuli. Layers and layers of organization are replaced in Southwest's business structure by spontaneity.

There's a story they like to tell at Southwest about Chris Wahlenmaier, his mother, and his boss. Chris, it seems, had just come from presenting what he thought was a terrific idea to a curmudgeonly sort of upper manager in the form of an Executive VP. The idea was turned down and Chris was walking back to his office when his mother, who was visiting him at the time, asked him in the hallway what was wrong. While Chris explained, a co-worker overheard the situation and said, "That's not right." Then he turned to Chris' mother and said, "You go down to that man's office and tell him you're upset that he didn't listen to your son; that your son has a good idea and he should listen to him." Chris' mother did just that. The manager's eyes opened wide, his jaw dropped visibly, and silence followed; then he broke out laughing, called Chris back in, listened more intently, and the idea was implemented. This story of spontaneity within the corporate structure is also an example of how Southwest manages up. Managing Up means that everyone's ideas are valued and that plans and behaviors often come into being not from committee but as a direct result of the person who creates them initially for his or her own use.

Recognition Cards are brightly colored business-card-sized compliments that each employee receives when he works at Southwest. These cards contain compliments such as: *Thorough: Completes a detailed task with quality*; or *You're a Joy to be with*; or *Enthusiastic: Happy and excited even when others aren't!* Employees are encouraged to give them out to other employees (or even customers) when the time seems right. The concept, now system-wide, was originally started by one employee who created them so she could spontaneously show her co-workers how much she respected them. It is common to see Recognition Cards taped to computer monitors and tacked to bulletin boards in Southwest offices throughout America.

TJ LUV PRESENTS: A Guide to In-flight & Gate Games is a collection of individual success stories of how individual employees have solved problems, created lemonade from lemons, and generated fun for customers who might be in boring or flight-delayed situations. This pack of 4"x 5" cards connected with two rings, was authored by three employees and is now presented by the People Department to new employees with this message: "Having fun is what made us number one with our Customers. Having fun is what gets us through the day, and having fun is what separates us from the other dull carriers! In fact, it is one of our competitive edges. So, pull yourself out of the dredges and into the competitive edges and Have Fun!"

If you've ever seen a Southwest Airlines television commercial, then you know this company values fun. I was fortunate to be able to view a collection of their best commercials from the last thirty years and I was struck by the fact that everyone of them used humor to deliver its message. Often, Herb Kelleher would appear, only to be drenched by a bucket water in the style of football players soaking their coach after winning a big game; or wearing a paper bag on his head with two eye holes cut out à la the New Orleans Saints' Unknown Fan.

Humor and fun are extremely important to the success of Southwest Airlines. They're important to their external message and they're important to the internal functioning of the organization. When Southwest started its Symbol of Freedom to Fly external advertising campaign several years ago — You Are Now Free to Fly About the Country — they also started an internal promotional campaign based on freedom. You have the freedom to make a positive difference; the freedom to pursue good health; the freedom to create financial security; the freedom to travel; the freedom to play and work hard; the freedom to learn and grow; the freedom to have fun; the freedom to stay connected. These people-related freedoms were accompanied by one of the more serious, yet heart-warming documents I've seen come out of Southwest — A Symbol of Freedom. Done up like a recently discovered parchment, this six paragraph poster succinctly describes what it means to work for Southwest Airlines:

"In the past, the skies belonged only to a few. Only those who achieved status achieved flight, because only the elite could afford the freedom to go, see, and do at a moment's notice.

"You work for a company of people who changed all that. You work for a company who believed then, as it does now, that flight should not be limited to the well-to-do, but that it should be an opportunity for all: That people should have the freedom to fly.

"Our battle for this freedom began nearly three decades ago. And while our maiden flight may be credited to only a few, our gallant mission belongs to you. You make that freedom possible. For thousands of people to go, see, and do, you make that freedom possible.

"By keeping our costs low, you make that freedom possible. By doing right by a Customer, you make that freedom possible. By winning a fare war or battling other airlines who'd rather see us go than come, you make that freedom possible.

"It is your spirit and tenacity that has made Southwest Airlines a Symbol of Freedom. Because of you, today, someone has visited a grandchild, explored an opportunity, or just taken a trip for no more reason than to see what's out there.

"Because of you, today, someone has the Freedom to Fly."

SOUTHWEST AIRLINES
A Symbol of Freedom

In the past, the skies belonged only to a few. Only those who achieved status achieved flight, because only the elite could afford the freedom to go, see, and do at a moment's notice.

You work for a company of people who changed all that. You work for a company who believed then, as it does now, that flight should not be limited to the well-to-do, but that it should be an opportunity for all: That people should have the freedom to fly.

Our battle for this freedom began nearly three decades ago. And while our maiden flight may be credited to only a few, our gallant mission belongs to you. You make that freedom possible. For thousands of people to go, see, and do, you make that freedom possible.

By keeping our costs low, you make that freedom possible. By doing right by a Customer, you make that freedom possible. By winning a fare war or battling other airlines who'd rather see us go than come, you make that freedom possible.

It is your spirit and tenacity that has made Southwest Airlines a symbol of freedom. Because of you, today, someone has visited a grandchild, explored an opportunity, or just taken a trip for no more reason than to see what's out there.

Because of you, today, someone has the freedom to fly.

Unconvinced about the success of Southwest's Fun/Work Fusion? Consider this formidable list of achievements: 1999's year-end results marked Southwest's 27th consecutive year of profitability. The DOT has listed Southwest as the dominant leader in ontime performance, baggage handling, and fewest customer complaints during the decade of the1990s. In 1996, Southwest created Home Gate, a system for home ticket purchase via the Internet; by 1999, 25% of its passenger revenue derived from www.southwest.com. *Entrepreneur Magazine* named Southwest the best low-fare air carrier in the Business Travel Awards in April 2000. *Fortune Magazine* named Southwest the best overall airline in 1996, and in 1998 ranked them the number one best company to work for in America (4th in 1999, 2nd in 2000!) And the list goes on.

But the most important way to judge success is by what people say.

Southwest keeps what it calls Good Letters. These are letters from customers thanking them for outstanding service, for thoughtful employees, for going the extra mile. Of all the Good Letters I was privileged to read, I thought I'd share this one with you:

"Dear Sir/Madam: I have a humorous story that I would like to tell you. On Thanksgiving Day I was flying to be with my son and family in El Paso. I left early (6:30 a.m.) so that I would arrive in Texas by 9:30 a.m. to start dinner. Of course Grandma has to fix dinner, right? I was carrying the turkey (unthawed and ready to stuff) along with the pies. I happened to find the ideal box and carefully packed the turkey and pies and carried them as a carry-on. I sat in the front row of the plane with the box between my feet not knowing where exactly I was going to place this package. A moment later, a good-looking, tall, black (for matter of identification only) pilot came forward and said, 'Ma'am, you're going to have to find some place for that box.' I said I know. He said, 'What about the overhead?' I replied, 'I can't or the pies will be destroyed.' He said 'We'll find some place for it.' Moments later, the flight attendant came along, same lines. I said, 'I know.' Just then the pilot came out, picked up the box and strapped it in the jump seat in the cockpit, and my turkey and pies flew first class to El Paso.

"I am a frequent flyer on Southwest and log a lot of miles during the year. One of the reasons for this is because of the laid back attitude of your employees. I work in a high stress job five days a week, and when I travel, I want it relaxed.

"The story has been told to numerous people who have gotten a chuckle out of it and repeated it to their friends. But then, the radio station I listen to in the morning was having 'Santa in the Cockpit' stories. Of course, I had to call in and relate my story. So, you have gotten good 'mileage' from one good deed! Thanks Southwest for all you do and for your friendly employees.

"I told the pilot 'Thank You' a couple of times; but, if it's possible to reiterate it one more time from your end, I would appreciate it. We have employee recognition awards at our work place when an employee goes the extra mile. If you have something like that, could this cute pilot be recognized? If not, next flight I'm on with him, I'll bring an extra pie!

"Sincerely, Kathleen Johnson"

There are many similar stories of Southwest employees thinking quickly, acting independently, solving problems logically, and not falling back on company policy. I am firmly convinced that Southwest's success can be laid directly at the feet of the kind of employees they have, the kind they seek out, and the SWA, which values spontaneity over rules. I am not alone in my beliefs.

"We have to remember," Colleen Barrett says, "that the other guys can match our fares; our frequencies; our equipment; and our facilities — but to date, they have not been able to match our high-spirited, energetic, enthusiastic, warm and caring, customer service-oriented people. We need to stand on our heads to assure that that fact remains in place!"

It's this spontaneous, out-of-the-box thinking in support of their business plan (low cost, on time, point-to-point service) that has made, and continues to make, Southwest the leader in the business of aviation. But it's also created what truly makes Southwest a Fun Works living laboratory of Spontaneous Fun.

Herb Kelleher best sums up Southwest's attitude this way: "We take our competition seriously, but not ourselves."

■

Update: 2006

What stories can be told about the most successful airlines in history? What stories that will validate the effectiveness of its culture of Capitalize on the Spontaneous? As one might expect, there are many stories created by the success of Southwest Airlines.

Financial success is always compelling.

As of June 30, 2006, Southwest Airlines reported second quarter income of $333,000,000 ($.40 per share), double their profits from the previous quarter. Not bad for any company and especially good for an airline in an industry beleaguered by 9/11, Hurricanes Katrina and Rita, and rising oil prices brought on by Middle East instability. How good was this report? While their main competitor reported only one quarter of profitability in the last five years, the first quarter of 2006 represented 60 consecutive quarters and 32 consecutive years of profitability for Southwest Airlines and for its stockholders. (Virtually every current and past SWA employee hold stock.)

Compelling also is the average 78% capacity on each of the more than 3,100 flights daily to and from 63 cities in 32 states, carrying approximately 90 million passengers per year. Compared to their first day in operation, the 436 Boeing 737s in Southwest's fleet represent an increase of 436 airplanes! Yes, that's right, Southwest began their first day in business with no planes in the air, on the ground, or even in a hangar!

Southwest Airlines' success has been so remarkable, in fact, that the US Department of Transportation has created a term, "The Southwest Effect," to describe what happens once Southwest Airlines enters a market. When Southwest Airlines enters a marketplace, the DOT says, competing airlines in the market cut their fares and increase the frequency

> "The journey has to be as much fun as the destination."
>
> MICHAEL FEURER
> OFFICE MAX

of flights. The cost of flying in that marketplace is reduced an average of 65% and the passenger traffic is increased an average of 30%. One market's passenger frequency increasing nearly five-fold after SWA entered. Herb Kelleher, Executive Chairman of the Board and Co-Founder, says that often people think Southwest is so successful because they only go into markets with high traffic demands. What he says eventually happens is that Southwest's low fares and good service create the demand. A month after Southwest started flights between Chicago and Louisville, passenger traffic tripled.

And what of their competition? First, competitors have sprung up out of nowhere, each trying to get their share of the low-fare, point-to-point market created by Southwest. And, like all good imitators, many tried to follow the Southwest Airlines model, at least as they understood it. But, for whatever reason, none to this date have been as successful. United Shuttle, Continental Lite, ValuJet, MetroJet, Delta Express, and ATA are gone. The futures of JetBlue, Ted, Midwest Airlines, and others are still in doubt. No doubt each was well-versed in the hard science details of cost, wage, frequency, etc., It is unlikely, however, that they were as well-versed in the soft science of creating and sustaining a culture similar to that of Southwest Airlines. The temptation in a start-up is almost always to focus on aspects of hard science, such as price. What many miss about Southwest is that while low fare is paramount to their continuing success, price is not *king* at Southwest. At Southwest, the employee is king. And when employee is king, then customers are treated well and low price works. And, success gets repeated — year after year.

Employees are always a source of good stories. Colleen Barrett started with Southwest as the legal secretary for Herb Kelleher. Today, Colleen is President of a company with more than 32,000 employees; a company consistently voted one of the Best Places to Work; a company that screens nearly a quarter of a million resumes every year to hire around 4,000 employees; and a company with the lowest turnover rate in the industry, 4.7%.

Deborah Stembridge, one of sixteen original employees, started as a Southwest Hostess, became a Cabin Attendant, and graduated to Flight Attendant. "The job kept getting better and better!" she said. Apparently, it's still extremely interesting and unpredictable. On a recent flight she discovered a pair of false teeth in the lavatory sink.

Rather than ask anyone or make a potentially embarrassing public announcement, she decided to walk slowly from the front of the plane to the back, making eye contact with every passenger and giving them a big smile. Three-quarters of the way through, a man put his hand to his mouth, jumped up, and ran back to the rest room. The passenger got his teeth back and kept his dignity because Deborah was spontaneously creative in her approach to solve the problem of the unclaimed dentures.

Stories like these support the success of Southwest Airlines, who, because of their culture, have been able to retain the essence of who they are in difficult and trying times. The Southwest culture contributes to its adaptability in good times and bad. Because they hire for character and attitude and train for skill, Southwest's culture is continually infused with employees who perpetuate their formula for success: keep it simple, keep it fun, share success, be spontaneous, make things happen.

But of all the stories that support and reflect the continuing success of Southwest Airlines, the one that means the most to me is the one that happened to me.

It was October, 2001. The tragedy of 9/11 was still brilliantly burning in everyone's minds, especially in those of us who were among the first few to resume flying across America following the country-wide grounding of airplanes. I was going from Cleveland to New York. Because of the existence of a federal law that essentially prohibits Southwest from selling connecting or straight-through flights, I had to go from Cleveland to Baltimore and change planes to fly to Islip, Long Island, New York, from where I would take ground transportation to the city.

As I waited in line in Cleveland to claim my unassigned seat, I looked around at the passengers flying with me. Because of the recent terrorist attack, few people were yet willing to fly. I learned later that Southwest President Colleen Barrett had suggested to employees who had direct contact with passengers that they maintain some reservation in their normally irreverent interactions but not to give up their identity and lose all sense of fun altogether. Southwest's gate people and ticket clerks were friendly, but subdued. Passengers were the same.

After landing in Baltimore to change planes, I found myself once again in line, waiting to board for the last leg of my trip to Islip. As I often do between planes, I called my office to check in. "Where are you now?" Mike said to me, extremely agitated. "I'm where I should be," I replied a little too brusquely, "standing in line at Southwest in Baltimore. Why?" "Can you see a television?" he said. "A plane has crashed in Queens and no one knows if it was shot down or not."

I looked back toward the television suspended over the chairs in the waiting area and saw awareness spreading across the faces of my co-passengers as they watched the events playing out live on national television. Today, we know the crash was not terrorist related. However, on that October day, mere weeks after the calamity of 9/11, none of us knew what to think . . . not that we weren't filling our heads with possibilities. None of us knew if this was the second wave of attacks.

I walked up to the woman behind the ticket counter to see if our flight was still going to take off. When she solemnly said it was, I wasn't sure if I was relieved or concerned. Maybe we'd all be better off, feel safer, if Southwest cancelled this particular flight, I thought.

I could see that the rest of my flight members were thinking similar things. The tone of the group, already subdued, became funereal. But our plane was taking off and we were going to soldier on.

As we began to board, what I saw reaffirmed my faith in the culture of Southwest Airlines. Without so much as a discussion, a prompting, a phone call, a message, an email, nothing, the gate attendant took it upon himself to look at each person's name on their ticket, and then use it while looking them in the eye and making a personal comment, such as: "That color blouse looks very nice on you, Ms. Yerkes;" "Looks like you got a shoe shine, Mr. Smith. Looks good." "Visiting your relatives, Mrs. Jones?" And so on. Each and every boarding passenger got a personal remark and a look in the eye.

As we walked down the jetway, a remarkable thing happened. We began to talk to each other, quoting what the gate attendant had said to us. "I noticed your shoe shine right away. It *does* look good." "So does the color of your blouse."

By the time we boarded, we were smiling and laughing gently. And we were talking. Instead of finding seats as isolated as we could, we continued our conversations and found seats next to each other. What had threatened to be a painful, scary experience had turned into a comforting, pleasant event. Because of their culture, Southwest Airlines had sought out and continued to nurture an employee who capitalized on the spontaneous and told us sincerely how good we looked at a time when we were scared to death.

Stories like these illustrate how important the culture of a company is to its continued success and to its ability to sustain itself through good times and bad.

I have no doubt as it faces continued competition, high fuel prices, and turbulent times that Southwest Airlines will continue to succeed and be a living laboratory for the success of the Fun/Work Fusion.

■

"Time flies when
you're having fun."

> "Corporate Culture does not compete with Business Strategy; it is the underpinning of success."

LESLIE YERKES

The Effectiveness Key

SINCE THE RISE OF SCIENTIFIC MANAGEMENT in the 1920s, we have been taught that efficiency is king. We have learned that time is money, that the system is the solution, and that the company has all the answers. We have treated the laws of Scientific Management as if they were the natural order of the universe.

Although the use of Scientific Management Principles in our work resulted in increased productivity, corporate growth, and increased wages and income, it also resulted in the segmentation of our whole selves, the minimization of the individual, and the elimination of fun from the workplace.

As we progress on the Timeline of Work Attitudes away from Scientific Management, we are discovering that paying homage to the god of efficiency inhibits spontaneity. And that limits our effectiveness.

Effectiveness is doing the right thing at the right time for the right reason. Effectiveness not only allows our whole self to participate in the work process, it requires it. To feel the satisfaction of making a meaningful contribution in our work lives, we must bring the best of our whole self to the endeavor; when we act effectively, we allow for and encourage spontaneity.

To capitalize on the power of spontaneity, we must balance our emphasis on efficiency with an emphasis on effectiveness.

■

"We grow up when
we have our first
good laugh at ourselves."

ELEANOR ROOSEVELT

4

PRINCIPLE FOUR
Trust the Process

YOU CAN'T MUSCLE ENERGY.
A LAUGH THAT IS FORCED IS NOT A TRUE LAUGH

There are two methods for managing events and companies: Task Orientation and Process Orientation. In America, we have perfected Task Orientation. We are makers of lists and studiers of time management. Our performance appraisals and reward systems are based on 'what' gets done, not on 'how' it gets done. We wrestle with ourselves because of our need for control. We manage daily to-do lists; we micro-manage employees and associates. We make things happen! But we do not always enjoy ourselves in our work.

Task Orientation requires control; control often limits fun.

Process Orientation requires trust; trust often encourages fun.

People are the backbone of Process Orientation and trusting them is the key to its success. Give people the big picture, describe your expectations, allow them to fail, support their efforts, celebrate their success, and Process Orientation prospers. The process makes things happen.

Trusting the process requires less energy and less supervision, is more liberating for everyone involved, and generates more fun and better results.

Trust your people and have fun in the process.

■

"I don't want to be put in charge of fun. That makes it a job and that would not be fun."

LESLIE YERKES

Employease
Inspiring Human Resources

When I walked into the room, the first thing I noticed was the diversity: young, old, black, white, Asian, male, female; the second thing I noticed was that no one was wearing a coat or tie; third, that everyone was smiling, laughing, and having fun. And when the meeting started, the room became a sea of whoops, hollers, and applause. The event was the monthly staff meeting of Employease, better known as First Friday.

It's during this two hour session that the 135 employees of this Atlanta-based company meet their new co-workers, hear the latest on the financial status of the company, and discuss a variety of issues that keep Employease a fun place to work.

Employease was formed in 1996 by then 22-year-old Mike Seckler and 23-year-old John Alberg, college friends who had an idea on how to better use the technology of the Web to help small to medium size companies deal with their overwhelming Human Resources problems. Along the way, the pair created an organization whose primary philosophy is this: treat people like adults and trust them to do their jobs. Their success on both levels has been staggering, so much so that people are flocking to Employease, looking to work for a technology-leading company and discovering that the atmosphere is even more advanced than the technology!

Employease is what's known as an Internet Business Service or, depending what you read, a pure ASP or application service provider. It was described to me like this. Unlike traditional software programs, which individual companies purchase, install, and manage on their own computers and networks, the Employease Network was built from the ground-up to live on the Internet. That is, companies don't need to install any software. They just pay a small per-employee-per-month fee to access the Employease Network via a web browser.

> "The only work that hurts
> a man is hopeless work."
>
> UNKNOWN

HR departments use the web-based program to manage HR benefits and payroll-related activities quicker and more efficiently. Employease customers report that they have cut the time they spend on administrative tasks by as much as 60-80% and now have the tools and time to focus on the more strategic issues of recruiting, motivating and retaining a world-class workforce. Mike says that has been the biggest benefit for their customers. "Employease Inspires Human Resources," he likes to say, quoting the company's tag line. This tag-line means two things for the company. First, they want to inspire Human Resources managers to become more strategic and secondly, they want to empower Human Resources managers to inspire their own human resources — the employees who make their company successful.

Because the program is web-based, anyone can access it without cost-prohibitive software. Employees and managers can enter, view, and edit information directly online from their desk or even from home within parameters set by the HR manager. Marital status, children in school, new family members, and other similar information can be directly inputted — no forms to fill out and get lost or be delayed; and no one has to spend time to handle the forms, either. This also frees up HR staffs to spend more time with what should be the focus of their jobs, the employees.

OUR VALUES

"We value a fun environment that inspires creativity. We value openness, honesty and integrity and will treat each other, our customers and our partners with dignity and respect.

We value inspirational, involved leadership with an honest style that instills purpose and trust."

— Mike Seckler

Because the insurance carriers, administrative partners, and other service providers are also connected to this program through the web, employee and benefit data can be handled much more effectively and reconciliation problems are eliminated via the electronic communication. In short, having providers, companies, and employees interconnected through one web-based program improves efficiency and effectiveness, and reduces costs. All of which makes working in HR in member companies a lot more fun.

But the real success story, in my opinion, is the quality organization that John and Mike created when they gave birth to Employease.

As a life-long business trainer, I have spent years guiding companies and individuals along paths that value diversity, encourage trust, and promote ownership. Imagine how it felt for me, then, to walk into a Fun Works living laboratory like Employease where all the concepts I have been seeking to instill in companies are alive and well and the very basis for their success!

Communication is one of the important values that successful companies share and at Employease that is best exemplified by First Friday. First Friday has been described as 'the meeting I never want to miss.' And I can see why. It's fun, it's open, it's information flowing free, it's respect, and it's a party. Needless to say, the staff loves it.

The First Friday meeting I attended was jammed. The room was so crowded that some of us were sitting cross-legged on the floor. But the atmosphere was electric. I'm sure you've had the experience of being at a national convention where management brings in a motivational speaker and everyone whoops and hollers and gets involved. Well, First Friday has that feel but it's organic, it comes from within as opposed to the applied emotion of those sales events. This is real and you can immediately tell the difference.

The first thing that happens is lunch — pizza and soft drinks buffet style, with everyone eating and talking. Then, the meeting is called to order, sort of, and this month's new employees are introduced. One at a time they tell who they are and why they've chosen to work for Employease. What's remarkable is that there's this common denominator that runs through their reasons — not only is Employease a high tech company that will allow them to showcase their abilities and satisfy their intellectual needs, but everyone described a way in which Employease would satisfy their emotional needs as well. John, one of the new employees, said it best. "I heard so much about this place, I just had to apply and see what it was all about. I've worked in a lot of places writing code, and writing code is what I love to do best. But this is the first place I've ever worked where they're writing code with a purpose — you know what you're doing!" At this point, cheers and applause interrupted his testimony. "And I said, 'this company is for me.' Thank you!"

At that point, the entire room gives John a standing ovation. I thought he might have gotten special treatment because of what he said, but each of the other five new employees received the same warm welcome including the standing O.

Phil, the CEO, who prefers to be called 'All Around Good Guy,' was next with the business update. "We manage by open book," he explained later. "We let everyone know our

financials. We trust them and they trust us. If our employees are going to truly be partners in Employease, then they have to be treated as such. They need to know where we are and what our strategies are and why."

Next on the First Friday agenda was Mike Seckler who discussed what branding means for the company. "A common misconception," he began, "is that branding is a marketing function." He then discussed how every customer has a 'moment-of-truth' when they interact with Employease, which either builds or damages the company's branding. And he emphasized that, because of this, it is imperative that every employee be a brand steward and deliver on the company's brand promise to 'Inspire Human Resources.'

"As you know," he began, "Employease has never spent a dime on advertising." (Which is really remarkable when you realize that they signed their first client in the fall of 1998 and by June 2000, had more than a thousand companies enrolled!) "But now we've decided it's

time. So here's what we're going to do." And with that, Mike explained the concept of branding and the action steps involved in their program. He showed a slide presentation complete with photos of the early days and their subsequent growth, accompanied by the strains of "Anticipation" and "Mission Impossible." The performance was punctuated by the laughter, asides, and applause of the appreciative audience. Everyone was getting warmed up for the next part of the process: homework, of a sort. The employees were broken up into teams and given a piece of paper described as 'your elevator pitch.' What they had to do was write out a three or four sentence explanation, in their own words, of what Employease is. And then, so that they felt comfortable giving this spiel to anyone they might see in the future, they role-played their presentations. Upon completion of this exercise, each employee was given a T-shirt with Employease's new slogan imprinted on it: Inspiring Human Resources.

Now, I've been lots of places where employees are given T-shirts, and maybe 10% or so might, *might*, put them on. But by the time all the break-out groups had reunited, 95% had put on their shirt. And no one forced them to do it!

First Friday broke up, then, to more cheers and applause with obvious anticipation for next time.

The T-shirts made me wonder about the dress code. Business has long had its dress code — suit and tie every day. Recently there's been a change — Dress-Down-Fridays. What's remarkable to me is that even during this casual day, I can see the hierarchy exhibited in the dress-down clothes. I can still tell by who's wearing what, who is higher in the hierarchy. At Employease, it is impossible to tell. "We are non-judgmental here," Hilary, the Office Manager, said. "You won't find anyone saying or even implying that someone's clothing is inappropriate or unsuitable. We trust everyone to be adult and casual at the same time. We don't get anyone wearing anything risqué, or vulgar, or not clean. Because we focus on results and what the individual is achieving, we pay no attention to what they're wearing. That results in a casual environment and no ageism. You can't tell how old someone is by their clothing. People wear what makes them feel good and comfortable, all the while knowing that they are here to work, to achieve the results that are expected of them. Clothing isn't important in a hierarchical sense. If it's clean and comfortable, it's just fine."

The casual atmosphere is certainly one reason people like to work at Employease, but, as I found out, there are many reasons – and most of them are based on trust.

Ezra was a financial analyst at an international investment bank. "When I started there," he recalled, "they told me 'We pay you a lot of money but we don't have fun here. The client comes first, the company second, and you third.' I would come to work every day at 9 am and wait around until about 3 pm when my boss would give me an assignment that he wanted first thing the next day. It would take me until 10 o'clock each night to finish. I couldn't understand why I wasn't allowed to come in at two. But the bank felt they paid for me, they owned me. Here, I'm trusted to work when it's required. If I'm late because of traffic in the morning, no big deal. All I need to do is get my job done. This is a flexible work environment. I don't have face time. I can dress comfortably, and I'm responsible for myself. It's non-judgmental and the company wants me to enjoy myself. If I'm not having fun, they don't think I'm going to do my best work."

> "All that is needed to make a happy life is within yourself, in your way of thinking."
>
> MARCUS AURELIUS

Michael, the Direct Marketing Manager, had a similar story. "I started as a consultant here. I saw how much fun everyone was having, and how much they believed in what they were doing, that I decided I wanted to be here full-time. One night shortly after I started, my co-workers were going to the Braves game as a group, but I had too much to do and I told them I'd pass. A few minutes later, Mike S. came in and asked why I wasn't going to the game with them and I told him about my work responsibilities. Mike S. proceeded to help me prioritize my assignments and volunteered to come in the next several days to help me just so I could go to the game. It's the philosophy of Employease that everyone needs time off and that having fun with co-workers is too important to be replaced by working late. I went and had a ball. This is the first time in my entire career that I really believe in what I'm doing and what the company I'm working for is doing. I really want us to succeed."

Sam, the Manager of Development, talks about how the new economy is driving Employease. "The times, they are a-changing. This is more than just a new economy, it's more than thinking 'outside' the box, this is a whole new box! None of the old rules apply. You know, the parent-child philosophy of companies and workers that most older companies follow? We have a young mindset. We're not all in our twenties, but we think young. We're very focused; we're driving new technology from the ground up. This is an awakening. And we're all in it like a family."

Alicia, a Quality Assistance Manager, has some concerns that the family atmosphere will last. "When we were starting out, there were just a few of us. Now we have more than a hundred employees. We want to make sure that the family feeling that the company started with stays here as we grow. So we work at doing things that keep us together. We promote from within. And our promotions, compensation, and rewards are not standardized or scheduled. They're based on merit. In some companies, that could be a problem, but here

there's no jealousy. Everyone truly cares about you and what you accomplish. And that helps keep the family atmosphere."

Brenda, Vice President of Business Development, puts it all in perspective. "Our goal is to attract the best people and then keep them. Our philosophy is to get someone with the right attitude, someone who lights up during their interview, explain what they're expected to accomplish, and then get out of their way and let them work. Our attrition is extremely low. If you start with good people, you keep them."

The overall attitude I found at Employease was best summed up by the Vice President of Finance and Administration, Doug. "We accept all people in a very genuine way. We treat them like they're real and that creates the culture we have. Employease is a combination of people with HR experience and Internet/IT experience, of all different ages, races, backgrounds, sexes, and home states. But because we trust our employees to be accountable for their actions, be responsible for their results, and take ownership of their jobs, we get great results. Along with those results, we see another advantage — we have a culture with a low political presence. Politics erodes trust; trust erodes politics. Employease is as ego-less as any company can get, especially when you consider how much talent we have working here! Our work ethic says I won't ask you to do anything I wouldn't do. And I think, most of all, we embrace mistakes. We know that

success happens as a result of failure. You won't get killed here if you make a mistake. Own up, fix it, and move on. Life is too short not to have fun."

My overall experience at Employease makes it clear why people love to work here; I'd love to work here. Something that co-founder John Alberg told me bears repeating because I think it's a good summation of what kind of company Employease is, and what kind of a company all companies could be if they'd follow their example: "Successful management requires a lack of ego. Surround yourself with good people because it has a snowball effect. Good people give off more energy than they consume."

You can trust him on that.

■

Update: 2006

My work as a change-management, human resource consultant keeps me in constant touch with the world of Employease. Because I am a strong and consistent advocate of trust and fun, the benefits Employease offers clients are ones to which I am highly attuned.

When HR personnel at client companies spend less time dealing with the paperwork requirements of HR, they are able to spend more time on such things as recruiting, motivating, and training employees. The benefits to the company of extra attention being paid to the soft sciences are the sorts of things that help companies improve in quantum leaps.

While I personally do not interface with Employease, I see the results when HR professionals with whom I work discover that Employease has given them more time to work on activities that directly impact the growth of their companies.

The question on my mind as I began my research on Employease' last six years was: How did they manage to grow during the dot-com downturn when other dot-coms were going out of business?

"We had a few problems," Mike Seckler, Employease co-founder, told me. "Like everyone else, we had to deal with the economic recession the country went through following 9/11. We even had to lay off a few folks to stay afloat. During that period, we saw about a dozen of our competitors go out of business but we survived because we did the right things at the right time for the right reasons. One of the things we did right was that John and I hired Phil Fauver to be CEO, which is kind of like hiring your own boss. We did that back when John and I were only twenty-five years old. We saw that Phil had tons of experience running and growing a company like ours and neither John nor I did. Nor did we have any ego driving us to be kings. We simply wanted to do whatever was necessary to make this the best company possible.

"The future's so bright,
I gotta wear shades."

PAT McDONALD
TIMBUK 3

"I think the decision to hire in a CEO, and then the way we supported those employees we had to lay off (and the dignified way we did it) were some of the reasons we made it through that period of a bad economy. Interestingly, when the economy turned around those same folks asked to come back and work for Employease again. And we were overjoyed to have them."

Evidence of Employease' success over the last six years is abundant in other ways, too. In 2001, *HR Executive* named Employease the Top Product of the Year. In 2003, *InfoWorld Magazine* gave them the Deploy Rating. In 2004 and 2005, *Business Insurance* ranked Employease Number One Benefit Information System. In 2001, 2002, and 2004 *Forbes Magazine* called them Best of The Web in HR. In 2005 *Forrester* awarded them Leading Pure Play Hosted Vendor. In 2006, *Garnter* awarded them Leader Quadrant Midmarket HRMS Magic Quadrant Report. And in 2006, they received the Codie Award as Best Human Resources Solution.

In addition, Employease has been profitable every year since 2003, has seen 50% revenue growth year after year, and has delivered 35 consecutive quarters of revenue growth.

These impressive outcomes are the result of the intentions of Mike and John when they started the company: make it a friendly place to work with a family atmosphere; hire only self-motivated individuals who want to accomplish big things — then don't babysit them; hire skilled people with the right personality and attitude to fit into the culture; and most importantly of all, encourage people to have fun at work. "Fun is still high on our culture list," Mike says. "We have a superstar woman named Fannie Dorsey who runs our office. She gives off tons of positive energy to everyone with whom she interacts. She makes it fun to be here. We decided we needed to let her know how we felt about her so we had an "I'm a Fan of Fannie" day, complete with Fan of Fannie buttons, balloons, and cake. The management team took her out to lunch. Not only did Fannie have a great time, but so did everyone else. The event reinforced to everyone that great attitude carries the day at Employease."

Some other things haven't changed, either.

"We still have a casual dress code, although we do dress up when we meet with clients. We now have more than 200 employees so our Fun Fridays are no longer physically possible to hold every week. But when we do have them, they're still as much fun. We go out to Braves games and such but instead of the entire company doing it, which we could do when there were only 35 or so of us, we do it by departments. A little smaller in size but with the same feeling. I still hear how much people want to work for us. They think we're smart, which we are, and that Employease is a fun and great place to work, which it is."

So much so that Employease has an unheard-of employee retention rate of 95%.

As for the quality, success, and value of their product, not only do their clients love them, but so does their competition.

In 2005, ADP, described as one of the largest providers of a broad range of premier, mission-critical, cost-effective transaction processing and information-based business solutions, realized that Employease had developed one of the best and most sought-after HR Software as Service (SAS) products around. Because ADP's historic focus was on payroll and related services, HR was not a strong suit for them. So, when they decided to expand into that area of company service provision, they understood that it made more sense to ally themselves with an established leader in the field rather than try to reinvent the wheel. After researching the competition, they decided that Employease was a company they could trust to work cooperatively with — one whose goals matched theirs. ADP felt that Employease' process was strong enough to create a meaningful, profitable relationship, one from which both companies would benefit.

Employease also had to trust the process. They had to believe strongly in their ability to add value to their relationship with ADP and not be overwhelmed by this giant in the industry.

So with both parties agreeing to trust the process, for the next twenty-four months Employease and ADP became partners in providing both Payroll and HR services to each of their client bases.

Their mutual trust was well-founded and the experiment worked well. During their relationship, ADP came to understand and value the quality of Employease' services and the culture of their company. In August of 2006, ADP submitted a bid to buy Employease and fold them into their organization.

Employease co-founder Mike Seckler felt the merger would succeed with respect to both the hard and soft sciences of each organization. "We have been close business partners for two years. Our associates have been working effectively together and there is great evidence that both ADP and Employease employees would thrive in each others' cultures."

The future for Employease is yet to be told. While more than 85% of mergers and acquisitions do not achieve their intended goals because of a failure to address the cultural issues between the merging companies, those who know *these* two companies believe the future of Employease under the ADP umbrella will continue to be one of positive revenue returns and a continuation of a culture that keeps people wanting to be part of the process of Employease.

Trust me, I'm one of them.

The Trust Key

IF WE'RE GOING TO LEARN TO TRUST THE PROCESS, we're going to have to learn to trust. Trust is the assured expectation that someone will do the right thing for the right reason at the right time. It is the belief in a positive outcome. Trust is not an absolute but is relative; we have various levels of trust at all times about all things. The higher our level of trust, the more likely we believe in the outcome.

Fear and fun are the opposite ends of a continuum. Fear comes from low trust; fun comes from high trust. When we have high trust, we have fun; when we have fun, there is high trust.

The only thing that prevents us, then, from bringing fun into our work is fear; fear that someone will object, fear that we will be considered less than professional, fear that we will lose our capacity to be serious about our efforts. To counteract that fear, we must develop a higher level of trust.

Fear is often the thing that stands between us and what we want most. Fear creates a reaction that makes our desires elusive. What we want most is coated with our own fear. To reach our goals, we must trust in our ability to achieve them and not be put off by the fear that goals naturally elicit.

When we have fun, we have trust; trust replaces fear and allows us to have fun. To have trust, you have to believe in the future and have fun in the present.

■

"It isn't best that we all think alike;
it is difference of opinion
that makes horse races."

MARK TWAIN

5

PRINCIPLE FIVE
Value a Diversity of Fun Styles

WE DON'T ALL DO IT THE SAME WAY

Fun, joy, and happiness are universal concepts. An act of joy, fun, or playfulness extended to another will span generations, cultural differences, gender, and language. The simple act of a smile can bridge all divisions.

Not everyone, however, expresses joy and happiness the same way; not everyone laughs the same. Think of the wide variety of laughs you've heard in your lifetime — rolling guffaws, high-pitched giggles, machine-gun-like snorts. It's the richness of the variety that makes the sound of a happy audience.

Likewise, not everyone experiences or expresses joy and fun in the same way. Fun is not, nor should it be, one-size-fits-all. The wider the diversity, the more ways in which fun will occur, the more opportunities for everyone to experience it.

Imagine a feast of a dozen courses in which every course is exactly the same. No matter how tasty the dish, twelve helpings of it would become boring. Companies are like feasts — too much of the same thing gets boring. But when everyone is encouraged to bring of themselves, to offer up their glorious differences, then our feast becomes rich in texture, quality, substance, nuance, and most of all — fun!

Be inclusive and share your fun energy with all constituents inside and outside your organization. Diversity is the best way to maintain a healthy company.

Celebrate it.

■

What do Gen Xers want in work?
Most important was job security.
After job security:

    84% Meaningful work

    79% A job that allows time for personal
        and family activities

    76% A job that is fun

FAMILIES AND WORK INSTITUTE, "YOUTH AND EMPLOYMENT STUDY 2000"

Blackboard, Inc.
Changing Learning through the Internet

*"The significant problems we face
cannot be solved at the same level of thinking
we were at when we created them."*
ALBERT EINSTEIN

I could see the Washington Monument from the window of my plane as I flew into Ronald Reagan Airport in Washington, DC on my way to the Fun Works Living Laboratory of Diversity, Blackboard, Inc. I soon found myself driving past my personal favorite, the Lincoln Memorial. Lincoln is a role model of mine for persistence — having lost thirty-three consecutive times before he finally won his first election. As President of the United States, Lincoln helped us through our national conflict over slavery, which I like to think began the process of valuing diversity in this country.

Across the street from the Vietnam Wall, is another personal favorite — the 10-foot tall bronze statue of Albert Einstein seated on a wall in all his rumpled-shirt splendor. My memories of DC begin with a trip I took as a 10-year-old Girl Scout, visiting the requisite monuments and memorials, and include the dozen or more visits I've made as an adult. An adult, I might add, who on one of those trips spent 30 minutes seated in Albert's lap, contemplating the Universe!

Einstein's quote at the beginning of this chapter is one I use frequently in speeches and training sessions because I think it so aptly applies to strategic planning and creating change: to solve problems, we have to change our thinking. A corollary of Einstein's statement is: 'If you want to make a change, you have to do something different.'

I was reminded of these two quotes when I was reading an article that called Washington, DC the new Silicon Valley. The Washington of my past was the repository of history, heritage, and senior members of Congress making deals in smoke-filled rooms. The Washington of today splits its space and time with a new generation — energetic, youthful, and dot-com

oriented. A different direction is being taken in Washington as the direct result of a new generation doing something different, of a new generation thinking differently than the generation before them. It was clear to me that if I were going to understand this Brave New World, I would need to rethink my positions — change my perspectives. I would need to discover what it was these young people were doing in Washington, DC!

Two of Washington, DC's leading young people are Michael Chasen and Matthew Pittinsky. The two were consultants with KPMG in the Higher Education Division when they created Blackboard LLC to become the primary contractor to the Educause IMS online education standards project in 1997. Chasen was 24, Pittinsky 23. In 1998, they met seven people from Cornell who have affectionately become known as the Cornell Seven. The Cornell Seven had just created a software program that Chasen and Pittinsky realized could help them achieve their vision of transforming the Internet into a powerful environment for learning and teaching. The two groups joined forces immediately and formed Blackboard, Inc. which has become the leading Internet infrastructure company focused on the global higher education industry known as the dot-edu marketplace. Today, Blackboard, Inc. serves more than 3,300 educational institutions and more than 2.5 million users in every state and more than 70 countries.

What we're talking about here in simpler terms is the revolution that's taking place in education. As of the year 2000, more than 90% of college students were connected to the Internet.

Many of those students use their Internet access to do things we had to do in person: sign up for classes, check their grades, review lecture information, receive new assignments, send their papers in to their teachers, and a wide variety of other supplemental activities related to going to college. The majority of those interactions take place using Blackboard's software.

Internet access for students and teachers is not intended to replace in-person interactions. Classes still happen; students are still late to them or sleep through them! Final exams are still held in large rooms with the answers going in Blue Books. But the Internet has allowed the learning experience to change, to offer options, and best of all, to improve.

I started my working life as a K-12 Special Ed teacher, teaching developmentally handicapped students. It was work that was challenging; it was work that I loved. I found, however, that there were no standards for judging teachers and the quality of their work. I had fellow teachers tell me I was working too hard, that I should create one lesson plan and use it for the next ten years. That wasn't me. I was the kind of teacher who reviewed and revised her plans weekly. So, when I read about Blackboard, I quickly understood that here was a system that could help establish objective performance standards to ensure quality education. Here was a system that could provide access for educators to multiple media to accommodate a variety of learning styles; a system that would allow a teacher to constantly update her lesson plans and instantly disseminate that information to the students. I had to learn more about this new way of teaching and learning.

In everyday use, Blackboard makes it easier for students to access information 24/7, check the results of tests, and submit papers; for professors and teachers to update courses, give tests, and interact one-on-one with students via e-mail and chat rooms. Colleges and universities have the ability with Blackboard to customize their web site appearance to maintain their brand and to make the information provided proprietary.

Blackboard's success can be seen from the sheer number of institutions of higher learning which have purchased and mainstreamed the software — more than 3,300 in less than two years! And also from the well-known names in education who have partnered with them: Houghton Mifflin, Inc.; McGraw-Hill; Pearson Education; Harcourt Brace; Academic Systems Corp.; and Kaplan. Blackboard, Inc.'s economic partners include America Online, Dell Computer, GoNetwork, KPMG LLP, Microsoft, NextEd, Oracle, PeopleSoft, Sun Microsytems, and The TLT Group. Investors support Blackboard's success, too. More than $51 million in equity was raised in its first three years of business!

Now I knew what Blackboard did and how well it was being received. But the primary purpose of my trip to DC was to discover how Blackboard, Inc., the company, operated and why it was so successful.

During its first three years, Blackboard has grown from the original nine members to a staff of 211. The company occupies three floors of a building in Northwest DC and has a branch office in Boston, created specifically for the two Boston-based employees who had been commuting daily to Washington.

This is a high-tech company and it looks like it. There are more ports for computers than there are for phones. Even the conference tables have computer ports. The offices are filled with casually dressed young people, buzzing with activity that seems to the casual

observer to be like that of a beehive — lots of comings and goings with only the comers and goers knowing where they are headed and what they are doing. Instead of name plaques or painted signs, people at Blackboard have their offices identified by their names written in chalk on a classic, leather-and-wood-framed blackboard.

"This is an amazing place and an amazing opportunity," says Mary Greaves, a member of the marketing team and the winner of the 1999 Aurora Award for Best Testimonial Video. "Michael and Matthew set the tone. They know we don't all do things the same way. The goal is to get done what you're supposed to get done when it's supposed to be done. They feel that you know what you're doing. Go and make it happen. They like different opinions so they encourage you to speak your mind, to be a little outrageous. That stretches the envelope and better things happen as a result.

"This is still a start-up business and I'm a start-up kind of woman. I'm kooky and a little nutty. I've been known to get a piggyback ride down the hall, singing showtunes. But I can also sit in a meeting with Michael, and Matthew, and Lou and tell them I don't like something they've proposed for the company and they'll listen to me. They want to hear what I have to say. And what everyone has to say. They like that we're different people and we see things differently.

"I'm the same with my team. I want them to talk back to me. Not in a negative or sassy way, but tell me what they think. To let me know when they don't agree. We're all hired to make things happen and you can't make things happen by just sitting there and doing what you're told. This isn't corporate America."

"Not only is it fun to work here, but it's fun after work. We work hard and we party hard," says Courtney Caro, another member of the marketing team and Mary's office buddy. (Working at Blackboard is like living in a college dorm. Two people are assigned to each office and they become office buddies.) "I'm in charge of trade shows, conferences, company picnics, and internal parties. I try to make our external events as fun and interesting as they can be. And our internal events are wild. Every Friday we have something we call 'Well-Dressed Burrito Day' where we go out

"Anything on earth you WANT to do is play. Anything on earth you HAVE to do is work. I never worked a day in my life."

DR. LEILA DENMARK, AGE 100

to eat burritos with the works for lunch. Then, after work on Fridays, we get together downstairs, have a few drinks, and dance. Blackboard is known for having a great product, great people, and great fun.

"We've taken the lead in the industry by holding our annual 'Blackboard Summit' to which more than 350 educators, legislators, and vendors show up. Our 2001 Summit is scheduled to be held in Berlin."

Lou Pugliese, CEO, came to Blackboard with a variety of experiences in cable and broadcast education, including being the Vice President of Turner Education Services in Atlanta where he was responsible for launching CNN Newsroom and a variety of educational ventures. "The Blackboard Summit is a unique and important forum in education," Lou says. "It has been recognized as an industry greenhouse of discovery and innovation, designed specifically so leading experts in Internet-based teaching and learning solutions can meet and share their ideas. For many of them, the Blackboard Internet infrastructure has been the organizing principle for online learning.

"It's our mission to become the Internet platform of choice globally for higher education online. Right now *blackboard.com* is the largest destination site on the Internet for creating and taking online courses."

"We are serious about becoming not only the leader in online education services in this country, but all over the world," says cofounder Michael Chasen. "Before Matt and I started Blackboard, we were both members of KPMG Peat Marwick's Higher Education Consulting Practice. That was the world's largest professional services firm serving colleges and universities. I'd like to see Blackboard achieve that status in our field.

"We know to do that we've got to have good people. We want to strive for diversity because we know you need to see things from different points of view. We encourage our employees to speak out and let us know what they think. We also encourage them to have fun at work and after work. We work hard, we should play hard."

"I was doing research at the Harvard Graduate School of Education when I became interested in trying to make the Internet a powerful environment for learning and teaching," recalls Blackboard's other cofounder, Matthew Pittinsky. "Part of our strategy calls for me spending as much time as possible with faculty, students, university CIOs and others in order to align us with the business, technical, and pedagogical needs of educators. So, I'm often out of town. I look forward to getting back here to be with these people. They're fun and this is a dynamic and energizing environment. I try not to miss our Friday parties if I can help it!"

"I used to work for the law firm that supports Blackboard," recounts Meredith Mayer, assistant to Chasen and Pittinsky. "It was so exciting when I'd come here and Matthew is so inspiring and passionate about the success of Blackboard that I just had to be part of it. It's really hard work and challenging but Blackboard has totally taken over my life. All my best friends are here. We're always together, even after work. This is a great company and it's doing well, so that's really rewarding — being able to work for place you enjoy and helping it succeed. I can't wait to come to work every day."

"I used to work for the same law firm," adds Shelly O'Horo, assistant to Lou Pugliese. "After she'd been here for a year, Meredith told me how much I'd like it so I took the job as the assistant to Lou Pugliese. Lou is recognized as the thought leader in the industry and I'm a real Southern Girl with a honey-sugar kind of pinch-you-on-the-butt attitude. There are so many different kinds of people here yet it seems to work. We all get along fine. I like to think of Blackboard as the Microsoft of the education industry. Only I hope they don't try to break *us* up!"

"When I interviewed for the job here," says Robert Jones, Director of Marketing, "I was scheduled to meet with Matthew at 7 p.m. I thought that was kind of a strange time but that

I'd go anyway and see what it was all about. When I got here, Matthew was playing Foosball with two other guys. That was my first impression. They didn't need to say that fun was important. It was obvious. Fun at Blackboard is accepted in any shape, any size, any form, at almost any time.

"Our attitude comes from Matthew and Michael and it's reinforced by the kind of people they bring in, both youthful and experienced. Our culture was set when we only had about 20 people. It's so much fun and so inspiring to work here that I don't think of this as a job, but more like a hobby. I like the people and I like to socialize with these people. I know it could change as we get bigger and need more structure but we'll try to maintain the fun atmosphere. Our company is becoming much more diverse yet the culture has stayed the same. As we grow some people will want to continue to go out, to get together for our Friday night after work Happy Hour, some will want to go home. We just have to accept all points of view. What we know is that fun doesn't hinder productivity. It helps it.

"We also believe in casual dress. It gives you greater leeway to create your own impression. It's about the contribution you're making, not about the clothes you're wearing while you do it. If there's a hierarchy, it comes from your performance and your merit. You are known for your successes, not for your title or what you wear."

"Work is not just a means to an end here," states Carlos Contreras Stefannoni, International Sales. "It's about having fun and being successful at the same time. It's not just laughing and doing crazy things, it's the challenge of how to grow our markets. We are currently Number One, but there are so many nipping at our heels. We have to work hard, be creative, and have a good time doing it."

"I was one of the original Cornell Seven," recalls Dan Cane. "We had a great idea back when we created the software but what's happened since we joined with Matt and Mike is beyond my wildest dreams. Blackboard is going to be able to extend education and learning beyond the classroom. It will make it possible for individuals to learn anytime, anywhere."

"I think our success is due to the people who work here," states John Simmons, International Sales. "These are very passionate people who take ownership of the company's success. They act as if the company were their own. That's the reason we've done so well."

"I think John's right," agrees Michael Stanton, Director of Investor Relations. "The secret of our success *is* the people. If you want success, assemble a great team to execute a good plan. A great team is one in which you value diversity, one that has an amazing variety of personalities. And if the attitude and the excitement are present, it starts to happen. And then comes success.

"When I came here, I had been with a New York City Internet company. I wanted to find a company that was addressing a huge market, was unique to that market, and that had a different and interesting approach. Blackboard was it. The higher education market in this country alone is currently $240 billion and the world education market will be $2 trillion in 2003. The Blackboard system is user friendly and is being used in more than thirty three hundred schools worldwide. And the people here are excellent. I couldn't have found a better work environment. There's something about coming in here each day that's infectious, that charges me up. I think it's the people."

Blackboard, Inc. is a company with a vision to change the world in a way that will foster even more change. That vision is to improve education. It's a change that will bring students and teachers closer together academically and help set standards for education that can be baselined and evaluated, something that will help teachers to become even better at their jobs.

There was a television commercial a while back in which a ten-year old boy was holding a thermometer over his bedside lamp in order to convince his mother he was too sick to go to school. The clever mother recognized the ruse and said he could stay home but that she'd get his homework assignments from the Internet. What was taken as a futuristic view of education then, will soon come to be commonplace if the diverse people and talents of Blackboard, Inc. have anything to do with it.

And I'm betting they will.

■

Update: 2006

I first discovered Blackboard doing my initial research for "Fun Works" when I came across an article that named the three-year-old company as one of the best and most fun places to work in Washington, DC. Reading that article prompted me to call them for a preliminary interview. My phone conversation supported my hope that Black board was, indeed, a "Fun Works" company and I was soon aboard a flight to our nation's capital. Upon my return, Blackboard's story became an official living laboratory for Value a Diversity of Fun Styles.

During the six years since our first meeting, I thought of Blackboard often. Would they survive the dot-com bust? If they did, would they take the company public? Would they become an attractive property to be acquired by a larger firm? Would they grow to the point where they would begin to acquire their competition? And most importantly, would their culture of fun and diversity be able to withstand the stress of growth? Would Blackboard still be, after all was said and done, a "Fun Works" company? I had to know.

I have kept track of Blackboard and the people I met there in a variety of ways. From reading press accounts I learned that co-founder Matthew Pittinsky was named the North-

ern Virginia Technology Council "Visionary of the Year" for 2001; that Blackboard won the 2005 Codie Award, sponsored by the Software & Information Industry Association, for the Best Post Secondary Education Learning Management Solution; that Blackboard was named to the Computerworld Smithsonian Collection of Laureates for Leadership in using IT to improve society; and that Blackboard was a finalist for both the 2005 American Business Awards for Best Support Organization, and for HR Leadership Excellence from the HR Leadership Awards of Greater Washington.

In person, I would meet Blackboard staff at the annual American Society for Training Development (ASTD) conventions. As Blackboard became more diverse, their marketplace expanded from their initial focus of colleges and universities to encompass the entire range of K-12, corporate learning, and e-learning opportunities. Invariably, the individuals I met at ASTD represented the fun culture I'd witnessed in person during my fact-finding session to their DC office in 2000. From those convention encounters, I felt certain that the growth Blackboard was experiencing hadn't eliminated fun from their workplace and culture.

From financial reports, I was aware of Blackboard's growth over the last six years. In 2005, they generated $136 million in revenue, $42 million net after taxes, and $14 million in earnings; employed nearly 800 at offices in Washington, DC, Boston, Phoenix, Vancouver, Amsterdam, Australia, China, and Japan; and had just consummated an agreement to merge with one of their main competitors, WebCT. That deal, combined with their continued aggressive sales record, would continue Blackboard's leadership role in the dot-edu market-place and give them a stronger presence in global education markets with an expanded international footprint in the UK, Canada, Finland, the Netherlands, Singapore, Spain, and Hong Kong. Blackboard currently has more than 3,650 clients in more than 60 countries worldwide, with more in the pipeline.

In 2003, co-founders Pittinsky and Michael Chasen took Blackboard public with an initial stock offer of 5.5 million shares at $14 per share, a total IPO take of more than $70 million.

From personal experience, I learned what it was like to use Blackboard's service. And I discovered how the process opened up my mind and made me think of various ways I could best use the interconnected community Blackboard generates.

I am an alumnus of Case Western Reserve University. And as such, I have always had the desire to teach at my alma mater. In 2004 I reached that goal when I was given the opportunity to become an adjunct professor at CASE Mandel School of Applied Social Science teaching one of my favorite topics, Change Management. As an adjunct professor, I, like every other professor at this august institution, was required, as they told me, to "…get on Blackboard."

Of course, I was excited. I was becoming an adjunct professor at my university, teaching a course dear to my heart, and I was going to experience firsthand what Blackboard was all about and what it means on a daily basis to faculty, staff, and students at schools worldwide.

My first assignment was to have my syllabus posted "…by Thursday." My problem was that I didn't have the first idea what this required. While I'm not a tech-geek by any stretch of the imagination, I can get around a laptop pretty well, thank you. But trying to use something new for the first time? I needed help.

Help came in the form of a less-than-ten-minute tutorial from Kristen Arbutiski, reference librarian at Mandel's Harris Library. I quickly discovered the site was easy to navigate, easy to understand, and easy to use. In twelve minutes my syllabus was up and I was on my way. But I wasn't done. Once I saw what *could* be done, once I realized I was part of an interconnected network of students and faculty and libraries and universities, I was energized. I spent the next several weeks planning what I wanted to include on my site. Students in my course are working professionals from all over the United States who fly in for weekend, accelerated classes. I could see many things that using Blackboard would to allow me to do, and I could sense it would allow me to do more things than I could think of at that moment. I'm even considering how I can use the Podcasting capabilities that Blackboard is making available at the end of the year.

The nature of Blackboard fosters community and connectivity, which allows me and my students to work together virtually; to get to know one another well before we actually meet in person; and to keep the relationship growing even when we are not sitting in the same physical space. That is the secret to Blackboard's success: giving all members of the community total access to to all the elements of an institution at any time and from any place on earth.

In my research for this update, I discovered two more examples of Blackboard's culture at work. The first has to do with Katrina.

Katrina's effect on the lives of those in the Gulf Coast has been well documented. One facet not often considered is the impact the storm had on education and on the students whose schooling has been interrupted. Keenly aware of the situation and the consequences, Blackboard created a central online hub where people can share resources and information related to restoring teaching and learning in Gulf Shore communities devastated by the Hurricane. They also established a free hosted platform where instructors could develop courses online to be available for one year. In addition, impacted academic institutions were eligible to have their e-Learning programs hosted by Blackboard for one semester at no charge.

The second indicator in the marketplace of Blackboard's culture was the creation of "The Greenhouse Award." Each year, eight winning schools share a $50,000 award for using Blackboard's technology to create exemplary courses, excellent campus services, and commendable communities of practice. These educational innovations are then made available via Blackboard to any system that chooses to implement them.

> "Happiness is the absorption in some vocation which satisfies the soul."
>
> WILLIAM OSLER

My research showed me that in the last six years, Blackboard has weathered most of the storms and survived most of the pitfalls encountered during the growing pains of a start-up company. They have succeeded financially, they have dominated their industry, and they are growing rapidly. To prove their ultimate success, I still needed to know the answer to this one question: Was it still fun to work at Blackboard?

"It's still definitely fun to work here," Colin McLetchie, Director of Talent Development and Employee Relations. "We're so big we don't have well-dressed burrito day anymore but instead we have fun runs, and desserts after work, and we go out to dinner. Though we've grown to seven floors in this building, we still partner office space, two to a room, because it creates camaraderie and collaboration. As we grow, we are strongly focusing on sponsoring diverse

events that will support the vision and mission of Blackboard. We have three goals we think will enhance our corporate culture and foster a positive work environment.

- Nurture greater understanding of the diverse cultures and communities represented by our employees,
- Provide fun and creative social and cultural opportunities that promote interaction across departmental lines,
- Further the cause of education in the local community by serving as a channel for community outreach and charitable giving."

In the six years since "Fun Works" first came out, the terms of the discussion in the academic and professional world have changed. The world is less concerned with the word *fun* and more concerned with *soft science*. In business, *hard science* is the physical process of what you do: production quality, manufacturing capabilities, financial planning, etc. The *soft science* is the culture of a company: Is it a fun place to work? Do people get along? What does it feel like to work there? Stated in the new terms, Blackboard is clearly still a leader in the hard sciences as well as in the soft sciences. Blackboard works hard and plays hard. For their more than 800 employees, the work at Blackboard is still fun.

Blackboard is a success. Founded on a solid idea supported by a unique and proprietary software system, Blackboard is growing and expanding and has become the acknowledged and undisputed leader in its field.

Most importantly, Blackboard is still a fun, diverse place to work.

■

"Happiness is not a reward —
it is a consequence."

ROBERT G. INGERSOLL

The Challenge Your Thinking Key

BEFORE WE CAN VALUE A DIVERSITY OF FUN STYLES, we have to challenge our thinking. We should understand that if there is more than one way to have fun, then there is also more than one way to work.

How do you know if your thinking needs to be challenged? Do you say or think: 'That isn't how I was taught!' 'I wouldn't do it like that!' 'That's the way we've always done it!' 'That's how we do it in this company!' If that sounds like you, or if you believe in unalterable, eternal absolutes, then you're probably a candidate to challenge your thinking.

As we progress along the Timeline of Work Attitudes and examine what we believe and why we believe it, it becomes clear that attitudes have already changed. Those of us who are in our 40s, 50s, and 60s have a mindset about our jobs that says we should work hard and follow the rules; that the harder we work the better off we will be. Those of us who are in our 20s and 30s denounce work for work's sake. Today's workers demand meaningful and challenging work in environments that enliven innovation, respect relationships, and reward results.

Our world of work is changing, like it or not. If you believe today like you did twenty years ago, then the time to challenge your thinking is now.

In the past we believed that if we behaved in a certain prescribed manner, we'd become successful. The mantra for today is: 'Examine first where you want to go and then choose the best way to get there.'

To get the results you seek while you integrate a diversity of fun styles into your work, challenge your thinking.

■

"All work and no play
makes Jack a dull boy."

ENGLISH SAYING

PRINCIPLE SIX
Expand the Boundaries

DON'T MAKE RULES THAT LIMIT THE PROCESS

The ideal balance of fun and work can be achieved when all individuals understand the boundaries of the work 'playing field.' Boundaries are not meant to constrain or inhibit individual contribution but rather to allow talented and well-intentioned team members to have as much autonomy as possible within the bounds of responsible fun/work.

Hold the container too tightly and you restrict the flow; operate without a goal or clear expectations and the results might not reach the mark. When we constrict boundaries, often the first element of a successful process to be squeezed out of existence is fun. Good boundaries create good balance.

To find the balance means wrestling with our issues of control. High control is the 'dark force' when it comes to the Principles of Fun/Work Fusion. Issues of control can crush or strangle the natural energy that gives life to invention, productivity, and prosperity.

To increase the possibility for the full utilization of talent, learn how to develop clear expectations, craft challenging goals, and set boundaries that are expansive. The more expansive the boundaries, the more room there is for fun to exist and then to grow. When fun is integrated with work, the better the experience and the better the result.

Expand the boundaries and watch your company grow.

■

"Imagination is intelligence having fun. Imagination is more important than knowledge."

ALBERT EINSTEIN

Process Creative Studios, Inc.
A better way of doing things

"Before I built a wall I'd ask to know
What I was walling in or walling out,
And to whom I was like to give offence.
Something there is that doesn't love a wall,
That wants it down."

"MENDING WALL" BY ROBERT FROST

When I think about the division of work within a company or an environment, I often think of this verse from Robert Frost. I realize that people feel the need for walls, for boundaries, for rules. We like to know for what we are responsible and we need to know how far we can go — what's expected of us both positively and negatively.

When I began my research into Process Creative Studios, Inc., an architectural firm in Cleveland, Ohio, I quickly discovered that setting boundaries in this company made them what they are and positively impacted on their external design success as well as on their internal company success.

Boundaries typically divide work. At Process Creative Studios, boundaries allow work to overlap, to let people into areas in which they are interested and in which their efforts show positive results.

Scott Richardson is a designer and co-founder of Process Creative Studios, Inc. He does exciting initial sketches based on listening to the client and drawing what he hears them describe. "I love when I share a drawing that has captured all the divergent ideas," Scott says, "and then I see the reaction, the spark in their eyes, when I have captured their big ideas and understand what they wanted to convey."

In the next step of the process, Richardson creates wonderful, full-color renderings with a three-dimensional feel. In many architectural firms, the involvement of an illustrator would end here. But with the encompassing, rather than restrictive boundaries that define Process Creative

Studios, Richardson stays with the architectural design and creation process all the way through until the end, listening, interpreting, and adding visualization to detail. It is this 'process' that gives Process both its name and its mode of being.

"Process approaches its projects in two distinct ways," says co-founder and designer/architect John Williams. "First, we do not define a line where architecture stops and interior design begins. We approach design in a more holistic, or European manner; design is simply problem solving. Whether applying this approach to something as small as a spoon or as large as a city, the basic concept is the same. In that regard, our strength is in designing the whole environment, from the smallest details in finishes and graphics, to the sculpting of the largest spaces and forms.

"Second, Process works with clients in a way that our name suggests. We do not present a design to a client for approval; we work with the client to develop the solution. The client is very much a part of the design process throughout the entire project."

Renata Rottinger came to Process with a dozen years experience in retail and restaurant design for Universal Studios, General Mills, First Union, and Ruby Tuesday. Her work for La Venezia Café (a unique, high-end restaurant in Winter Park, FL) was featured in the book *Cafés & Coffee Shops*. Yet Renata doesn't want to be walled in as a restaurant designer. "I like to do theme restaurants. But more than that I like perfect spaces. It's like a perfect song — when you hear it for the first time there isn't anything you could do to it to make it better. I feel like that about spaces when I walk into them and I know that's what I want to do. I don't want to be limited, I want to work on things that make me feel good."

> "To love what you do and feel that it matters — how could anything be more fun?"
>
> KATHERINE GRAHAM

Titles are another kind of boundary. The Process Creative Studios Professional Staff Listing gives no titles; business cards for all six members contain absolutely no titles. All are simply members of Process Creative Studios — there are no walls here, this is a team.

Evie Goslin, who provides full-time office assistance and drafting duties while she attends school evenings and weekends in pursuit of an architectural degree, describes Process as " . . . a relaxed atmosphere. This group works hard and cares about quality. They consider each job important yet they still find time to play — with the dogs, at lunch, after work at the brewery, and doing things together as a group. It's not work when we know each other so well, it makes things less tense."

Beth Graham, an interior designer, says, "Everybody knows everyone real well. We communicate well and we work well together. We care about the simple things. Because of the way this company is, we don't have to leave our personal life at home. The boundaries include the whole person.

"There are no silos here. No marketing division, no interior design division, no architectural division. We cooperate to see that the work gets done. We are a team; there is give and take. We've become work partners."

Process began as John C. Williams Architects in 1994, evolved into Process: An Architectural Studio in 1996, and became Process Creative Studios when Richardson merged his design studio in 2000. The resultant six-member firm understands process, and they understand fun.

Process Creative Studios is housed on Cleveland's near west side, across the street from the legendary West Side Market and next to the Great Lakes Brewing Company, legendary in its own right for its internationally acclaimed beers and the fact that none other than Eliot Ness dined and drank in the establishment that occupied this space during the 1940s.

When I entered their offices, I was greeted by Spalding, Jackson, and Spree who bumped my thighs with their noses and begged me to play catch. Spalding and Jackson, you see, are Williams' Weimaraners, a daily presence in the office; Spree is Richardson's Greyhound, a frequent, but not constant, presence. "Spalding and Jackson are part of my life," Williams explained. "I don't want to leave them at home alone all day so I bring them to work. Now, it's a normal thing for them to be here. Our clients have come to expect to be greeted by them and often they will bring a treat or two with them; funny, they don't remember to bring a treat for the rest of us!"

Spalding, Jackson, and Spree picked up their toys and we all went off to the conference room to talk about Process.

The first thing that Williams said was that upon reflection he wasn't sure his company deserved to be in a book called *Fun Works*. "We don't spin around on chairs here," he began. "We are serious about what we do." I quickly told him that the kind of fun we were talking about was not applied games or activities. What we were looking for was an attitude that made being at

---

"Whistle while you work."

THE SEVEN DWARFS

---

work a fun experience. John assured me that the process employed by Process made this a fun place to work.

"Then we qualify," he said. "My goal wasn't to create a standard, stuffy office with white shirts and ties. I wanted a place that would be a 'Gee, I want to work there' kind of place. That's why we picked this location and did the rehab design ourselves. We wanted the fourteen foot brick walls and the exposed ducts and beams. We loved the fact that it was an old

ballroom, and kept parts of the history of the space, while adding our own contemporary elements. I didn't want to create an environment that felt like there were too many rules."

Along with the design decisions and the inclusion of Spalding, Jackson, and Spree in the daily scheme of things, the office features seemingly unlimited M&M's and 'on-hold' music that is eclectic to say the least. "We like to select our on-hold music so it doesn't seem so canned. Like our design work, it says a little bit about who we are. We play artists ranging from Django Reinhart, Billie Holiday, and the Brian Setzer Orchestra to Morphine, Tom Waits, and Asleep at the Wheel. We've even played one of our client's recordings, much to his surprise. It's very entertaining getting comments from our callers, whether it's positive or 'change that music!'"

Like many of today's fun companies, Process has no dress code. "If you trust your people," John explains, "they will know how to dress appropriately." Another sign of Process' non-rigid thinking is the office hours, which are very flexible. "Everyone comes in on their schedule with total awareness of what needs to get done and their deadlines. When you trust people to discipline themselves they usually do a better job than when the discipline is applied. At least that's been our experience."

The impression you get of their office tells you all about the team — they are clean, organized, stimulated visually, casual, and fun loving. In short, it feels like a place where you'd say 'Gee, I'd like to work here!'

Even the restrooms are unusual. Instead of 'Men' and 'Women' or 'His' and 'Hers' or 'Ladies' and 'Gentlemen,' or any duo you can imagine, the restrooms at Process are titled

'Us' and 'Them.' "It's really fun to see how people deal with that," John remarks. "It's the sort of thing where there's really no way to make a mistake — unless of course, they choose not to go at all!"

Clients who choose to work with Process haven't made a mistake either. Not only do they get good people who love their work, but also they get quality results. In Process' short life span, they can count many well-regarded projects and awards including: the IIDA Award Winning Store, Planet Source; the Still Life Café at the Cleveland Museum of Art; retail prototypes such as E-Street Urban Street Wear and The Grand Prix Stores of America; and Century at the Ritz-Carlton Cleveland, a new direction for the Ritz-Carlton's food service branding.

"Century was a great project and a great challenge," Williams recalls. "The property owner, Forest City Enterprises, wanted something that recalled the train station that used to be the heart of Terminal Tower where this restaurant is located. The theme we all selected revolved around The Twentieth Century Limited, the classic bullet-nosed, Art Deco train of the 30s and 40s.

"In keeping with that theme, we had designed a curved reveal made out of aluminum to give the impression of being inside a dining car on the Twentieth Century. The contractor said it couldn't be done. We spent the better part of one morning explaining why we wanted the curved reveal and how it would make the diners feel. When we left the meeting, we were resigned to the fact that it wasn't going to happen.

"But because we had included the contractor in our discussion of why it was important instead of ranting and raving about why they *had* to do it, the contractor felt ownership and studied the plan and then came back to us and said they'd figured out a way to make it work. I'm certain that curved reveal is there today because we extended our boundaries and included them in the project."

Including coworkers, clients, and contractors has always been part of the process for Process. Everyone is involved from the word go; it's a direct result of having expansive and inclusive boundaries. "The client makes the project," Williams says. "I would rather pick the client than the project. Projects are just things. It's clients who make things happen; who make the experience good or bad. When you like your clients, it's easier to go above and beyond and make your best possible contribution. We try to have great relationships all around. Life is too short to have adversarial relationships. Rapport with the client makes it fun; we can joke and tease with them.

"The best compliment I have ever received," Williams recalls, "was when a client on a particularly difficult project said to me, 'This was fun. I'd do it again tomorrow.' That's our goal — do great work, have fun while you're doing it, and have the client love not only what you did but the process as well."

Even in something as serious as the process of providing input for the firm's five-year plan, you can see that the Process staff takes seriously its commitment to expansive and inclusive boundaries. While Williams and Richardson were working on the plan, Renata, Beth, Amie, and Evie were asked to submit their desires, goals, and expectations — individually, not collaboratively, to ensure that every member of Process had input into shaping its future. But as they thought about it, the four staff members felt that the team approach was more in keeping with the Process Way, and that the best manner in which to present the infor-

mation was to create a video. And so they did. It was their first ever effort and I was impressed with their story-telling ability, their insight, and the humorous way in which they did it. Spalding, Jackson, and Spree of course had lead roles, as did the M&M's.

Interspersed between their salient points (taking more classes, expanding boundaries further, more involvement in more projects) were out-takes, mocks on character habits like speaking too quietly, a running gag with the intercom from the front door that sounded strangely like the garble one hears at a fast-food-drive-thru, and the problems they had with having to spell the original company name (Process: An Architectural Studio) to people on the phone (No, that's the grammatical element colon not C-O-L-O-N).

Process Creative Studios is a Fun Works living laboratory of Expand the Boundaries. It is also a design studio operated by people who believe that good design is evocative, functional, and attractive; that good design challenges and involves risk taking for both the client and the designer. Process also believes that what they offer their clients is not a commodity but truly is a process, a process that engages their abilities and includes the client, the company, and outside vendors. They believe that by creating expansive and inclusive boundaries, and maintaining them like Robert Frost did in "Mending Wall" the process will be fun and the results will be the best they can be.

HAPPY HOLIDAYS

Photos by Eric Rippert

This quote from Henry Bertoia, one of the 'godfathers' of 20th Century design sums up Process' feelings about design: "The urge for good design is the same as the urge to go on living. The assumption is that somewhere, hidden, is a better way of doing things."

By creating expansive and inclusive boundaries, Process Creative Studios has discovered a better way of doing things.

And it's fun.

■

Update: 2006

I started this company because I couldn't find a place to work where I could be myself and still create quality design, where I could do great work and enjoy the process. I need serious work but I need to have fun, too," John Williams reminisced during our follow-up interview. "And nothing's changed. I would much, much, much rather do mundane work for fun people than do high profile projects with people who are difficult. Lucky for us, Process has it all: high quality work for people who are fun."

In the six years since I first visited Process, some things changed, some stayed the same. None of the five original staff members whom we had interviewed remained; all had moved on to other firms and other cities. The day I interviewed John for this follow-up, nine-year-old Jackson, one of John's Wiemaraners, was taking the day off from work to spend time with John's former wife. And four days before the interview, Spalding, John's other Wiemaraner, passed away at the age of twelve.

In the *same* category, Process was still doing award-winning work, the new staff tremendously enjoys working at Process, most of Process' clients were still clients, and M&Ms were still the snack of choice. In the *more-of-the-same* category, Process has doubled its volume, increased its profitability, now employs a staff of seven, and has increased its client list to include being the architect of record for Heinen's Supermarkets as well as winning the prestigious Thompson Hine LLP account.

Process was invited to be one of four architects to submit a proposal for Thompson Hine's $6,000,000 addition and renovation project. "We got a call asking us if we would be interested in vying for the project. I said we would and asked who our competition was. When I found out,

I laughed out loud. We were up against the largest architectural firm in Cleveland, the largest firm in Washington, DC, and the largest firm in America. I think we eventually got the account because, as it says in your book, we 'expanded our boundaries.' At the end of the interview, I took a chance, knowing full well that I might offend the review folks and lose the job, but I said to them I would feel insincere if I didn't say that I thought there were at least five other firms in Cleveland who could also do their project and that they probably didn't have to go out of town to find people to bid for their work. Once I said my piece, I got no immediate response and the interview ended. Several days later, I got a call that said we had gotten the project. I asked what the tipping point was and they said it was when I took the chance and told the Thompson Hine folks that I thought they should expand their horizons and look closer to home."

This is actually a good description of how John Williams has built Process: expand your boundaries in your own backyard. John's vision was never to build a company that would rival the size of any of the three with whom he competed for the Thompson Hine project. His intention was always to stay small and manageable, be the David against the Goliaths. He wanted a company where he and his staff could work unfettered in their own backyard. "We got an offer to do a project in Lima, Ohio. Now that's only four hours away but that's a problem. It's too far to drive and too close to fly. And because we are very much hands-on people, we would have to charge the client so much extra for travel time that it wouldn't be worth it to them. I recommended they find someone qualified closer to home. I guess that's sort of expanding the boundaries, too.

"Isn't it?"

One of Process' largest clients remains the $8 billion Cleveland-based Forest City Enterprises, a real-estate development firm with projects under construction from New York to Los Angeles. It was the Progress Century Restaurant project for Forest City that first caught my eye when I was doing my initial research in 2000. When I asked John about Forest City, he said he's never sought out projects to do, that he's always sought out companies that match up with Process' philosophy of being fun to work with and caring about the community. Which is why Forest City and their people get along so well with Process, John, and his entire staff.

But my attention became really focused when John told me about SchoolOne.

SchoolOne is a growing IT company that, among other things, connects students with teachers with parents with schools so that anyone involved in the process of educating a student can have access to all the information required, from homework to class assignments to grades. Started in 1999 in a 1600 square foot office in Westlake, SchoolOne quickly grew from 7 employees to a wall-bursting 65. "We simply had to move and we were looking for space in Cleveland. We found an ideal spot on W.25th Street," co-founder Michelle Tomallo recalled. "The unusual part of the space was that the landlord was an architectural firm that was planning to design a new space for themselves in the same building. My partner Micki

Tubbs and I were worried that we might get lost in the process so we took a chance and asked if they would allow us to use a different architect who would be able to focus all their attention on our needs. The firm was a little taken aback but we were given three names by the broker working with the landlords and us." The first company never returned our call, the second was scheduled for a 10:00 am meeting, and the third for a 3:00pm get-together the same day.

"On the day of the meeting, the 3:00 pm called and asked if they could move up our

meeting to 9:00 am because they had a client emergency that afternoon. We agreed.

"Halfway through our 9 o'clock meeting, I called back to our office and asked our receptionist to call the architect with the 10:00 am appointment and cancel. Our 9 o'clock meeting was with John of Process Studio. The first time we spoke, both Micki and I had an immediate gut reaction that these were the folks we were looking for. By the end of the meeting we were laughing and joking like old friends. So we agreed to work together on creating the headquarters for SchoolOne.

"Then came the real test of our relationship — the building we were to move into burned down seven weeks before occupancy. We still had an urgent need to find space but we had no place in mind."

"The City of Cleveland had been pitching us for months to look at the Idea Center in Playhouse Square," Micki recalled. "I didn't want to be in downtown Cleveland but finally I agreed to take a look. Like we did with Process, we had this immediate gut reaction and knew this was the place. John said he could get us the look we wanted and the contractor said we could be in and operating in sixty days. Amazingly, they were both right. We signed the lease on December 18th and took possession of our completed space on February 24th. We love it. Our employees tell us it's a place they're proud to come to."

John and Michelle maintain an ongoing business relationship that's connected by M&M's, dogs (SchoolOne has a chocolate lab named Pyper that greets guests at the door much like Jackson does), and a sense of humor.

"Our connection with SchoolOne was a great example of Expanding the Boundaries," John recalled. "Taking on a client who had a landlord that was a competitor is an unusual way to start a relationship. Then staying with them through the fire and getting them in place in sixty days was all way beyond the normal relationship. But Michelle and Micki are good people and everything just seemed to click. It was actually pretty easy."

The rest of the last six years have not been easy for Process. 9/11 changed how people did business and while Process lost staff during this period of country-wide downsizing, they managed to subsist. Eventually, they found good folks once again. "One of the people who worked here for a short while didn't understand our culture. He thought that the casual atmosphere meant we weren't serious about our work. But we are. We work hard, we have fun while we're doing great work, and we play hard, too. He thought we were living just the other side of the coin. What he didn't understand was that we are the whole coin. We are both fun and work."

After plateauing, Process has once again begun to flourish. In addition to expanding their boundaries and getting more clients closer to home, they have been recognized with several awards, including being chosen as a COSE Ten Under Ten winner — one of ten outstanding companies in Cleveland with fewer than ten employees. "I don't want to compete in size with big guys. I want to compete on the quality of work, but I want to stay small enough that I know everyone personally. That means a lot to me, having people who know you so well they know how to tease you."

John believes he was able to deal with some of last year's non-work problems because of the relationships he has with the Process staff. "We all get along so well," Natalie Pauken, architect/designer, says. "This is a fun place to work and I've learned so much since I've been here. I'm the serious one in the group. Sometimes, I feel like the punching bag. Whenever I bring up something, I feel like they all jump on me."

"That's because she's a mother figure," says Tiffany Beavans, designer.

"Natalie's easily the most mature of all of us," John chimes in.

We're sitting at lunch at The Great Lakes Brewery. John, Natalie, Tiffany, Steve Smrdel, and Therese Vitale are reminiscing about Tiffany's employment with Process. Tiffany has just gotten engaged and has resigned to move to Cincinnati in preparation for getting married. It's her last day and stories are flying.

"When I hired her, she told me she loved me and started crying," John says, matter-of-factly. Tiffany explains that she'd been trying to get hired as a designer at Process for several weeks. She was not happy selling furniture and wanted to use her design degree somewhere she could actually do good work. At her previous job, Tiffany had several working relationships with Process and desperately wanted to work there. "When John said I was hired, I was so happy I did tell him I loved him and I started crying."

Steve had an offer from one of Cleveland's biggest architects but he really wanted to work for Process. "I kept calling John, asking him if he'd made up his mind about offering me a job. I didn't want to have to take the job offer I had, I wanted to get an offer from the company I wanted to work for – Process."

"He was begging me," John says, and the whole staff laughs knowingly.

It's clear to me that there has not been any fall-off in the enthusiasm of Process' current staff since my last visit. "This is a great group," John says." They're the best."

It's also clear to me that John, at heart, is a GenXer, even though he's technically a boomer by age. John knows what a great work situation should be: "Work needs to be fun in addition to being challenging." Newcomer Therese, says it best. "To be fulfilled, we need to demand as much from the job as the job demands from us. That means it has to be fun, we have to learn new things on a regular basis, and we have to work with great people."

As the time came to say goodbye to Natalie, the group grew quiet. Then John said, "It just came to me, sitting here, that I hire employees the same way I look for clients. I look for the right kind of person with the right kind of character and personality. I can teach the skills they need to know, but I can't teach them to be good people. So I hire good people and train them."

In the last six years, John has become a race car driver, driving his Porsche Boxster S in SCCA competition. In 2005, John took twenty-seventh place in the nationals at Mid-Ohio in Lexington, Ohio. "Hey, that's great," John explains. "I started 38th, was knocked off the track and into a spin, and worked my way back up to 27th. And I only have one car on a trailer that I pull behind my SUV. Subaru has three semi trailers and dozens of crew. I guess I enjoy taking on the Goliaths."

John's goal for the next six years is to continue building Process while he takes more time off to race. He plans to do this by getting his staff more invested in the business and by continuing to create a culture of fun at work. "If I'm going to do more leading and still take more time off, I have to make sure these guys can run the ship without me. That's my goal: expand the boundaries again but in the process, maintain a culture that is both sides of the coin – fun *and* work."

■

The Time for Renewal Key

WHEN YOU EXPAND THE BOUNDARIES, make sure you include time for renewal. If we would let it, our work would consume us emotionally, spiritually, and physically. So that we don't get used up, we need to replenish our energies. We need time for renewal.

There are three ways that we replenish our selves: time, food, and fun. Take time during the day to break away from what you're doing. Take a short walk. Get a cup of coffee. Break the intensity.

Take time during the day to eat. Go to lunch; take a coffee break. The time off is as nourishing as the food. When you go to lunch, eat something. The benefit of stoking your physical engine while your brain is running in incalculable.

And enjoy yourself along the way. Make your time off doubly pleasurable by talking with someone you like. Share experiences. Exchange ideas. Have fun.

If your work itself is fun, then you will discover that you are replenishing yourself while you work. If your work is fun, it's less consuming. The ultimate fear we all have is burnout. We don't want to say: 'It got the best of me!' We want to give it our best, not have it taken from us. Take time for renewal.

How many of us feel like this? 'I was put on this earth to get work done. Right now, I'm so far behind I think I'm going to live forever!' We may feel like that but the truth is we will *not* live forever — but the work *will!*

If you find yourself at home after a long day totally wiped out, totally empty, with nothing more to give, you know how hard it is to get started in the morning. If you feel like your time at home is spent recovering from your day at work, then you need to set boundaries that will allow you time for renewal.

The sacrifice of your time and energy is not required to achieve great results. Set boundaries that allow time for renewal.

■

"Happiness exists when
the things we believe in
are consistent with
the things we do."

PRINCIPLE SEVEN
Be Authentic

BE TRUE TO YOUR BEST SELF AT ALL TIMES. BE CONSCIENTIOUS

Fun isn't something we can apply like a coat of paint. It isn't a suit of clothes we choose to put on because it's appropriate for the occasion. Fun is the way we really are; it's who we are at the very core of our being. The Wizard of Oz chose to project an image to his countrymen that he felt was worthy enough to be called The Great Oz; he hid his real self behind a curtain. In the end, it was not his image that held the seeds for success, however, but rather his authentic self that saved the day.

To be successful and to have fun at work, we need to be authentic. For a company to be successful, its employees need to be authentic. When we are under stress and duress, our real selves will out. If we are projecting a façade, it will crack under strain. If we are authentic, we will make the right decisions at the right time for the right reasons.

Authenticity cannot be learned, it cannot be faked. Being authentic requires us to be and act ourselves; it requires us to trust that who we are is the right person to be at the time. When we are authentic, we can trust our response to any situation. We don't smile because we should, we smile because we can't help ourselves. When we are authentic, we are our best selves at all times. When we are authentic, fun naturally integrates itself into our work.

To have fun at work, be authentic.

■

"Work is much more fun than fun."

NOEL COWARD

Isle of Capri Casinos, Inc.
Isle Style

When I arrived in Biloxi, I discovered it was shrimping season. My only experience with shrimp boats, I have to admit, is vicarious. Everything I know I learned from *Forrest Gump*. There, in the blue waters of the Gulf of Mexico, I saw those authentic, white shrimp boats with their jib-arms and pulleys and nets and I just knew I'd have to have some shrimp once I got to my destination, the Fun Works living laboratory of Be Authentic — Isle of Capri Casinos, Inc.

Biloxi, Mississippi is home to classic southern houses with deep verandahs, tall sweating glasses of sweet iced tea, gracious manners, and friendly folk who are as authentic and conscientious as one can be. A perfect setting for a perfect vacation; home of Isle of Capri Casinos gaming resort, part of the Isle of Capri Casinos' stable of one dozen such resorts.

The gaming industry understands its market as well as, if not better than, companies like Proctor & Gamble understand theirs. Gaming operates under the Pareto Principle, an economic law formulated in the 19th century by Italian economist Vilfredo Pareto, which says that 80% of your income comes from 20% of your clients. While the 80/20 Rule applies to virtually any business, gaming people seem to understand its ramifications and nuances better than most — the concept of the Preferred Shopper was virtually their creation. We've all heard stories about high-rollers who are picked up at the airport by limousines, whisked to totally comped penthouse suites, and plied with free food and drink. That's not an urban myth; it's true. The concept is simple: when you know which customers provide most of your income, treat them well.

The gaming industry is a leader in preferred-customer marketing. Isle of Capri Casinos, Inc. has expanded this concept to include more than 3 million players of all levels with a program called Isle Gold — a credit-card-style program that allows members to swipe a card to buy chips and markers, make a purchase, or

utilize their line of credit. Isle Gold allows not only high-rollers, but every level of participation to be rewarded appropriately by the company. As in all Preferred Shopper Programs, rewarding customers for their behavior encourages more of the behavior that has been rewarded. Isle of Capri Casinos, Inc., though not the largest, is considered one of the most innovative and fastest growing public gaming companies in America due in no small part to its unique brand and theme. And to its commitment to fun.

In 1990, Bernard Goldstein, a retired businessman who was looking for a second career and who was determined to have fun this time around, formed what would become Isle of Capri Casinos, Inc. His initial venture was a riverboat casino in Iowa, one of the first attempts at gaming under Iowa's newly enacted gaming ordinances. According to everyone's gracious evaluations of that venture, it was a failure. In 1992, he moved its riverboat, actually a barge, to Biloxi, Mississippi, and formed Casino America (later renamed Isle of Capri) where they corrected every mistake they'd made the first time around and embarked on what would become a highly successful corporation operating a dozen casinos, a race track in Florida, and a cruise ship out of New Orleans.

Isle of Capri Casinos, Inc. has become one of the darlings of Wall Street, going from $2 a share to a projected $19 a share in 2000, and from $800 million in earnings in 1999 to $1 billion in 2000. The CIBC World Markets equity research into Isle of Capri, Inc. on May 10, 2000 says, in part: "The Isle of Capri is a diversified gaming company that has implemented a strategy to build a strong brand name in growing secondary markets." "ISLE will have 14 properties in ten distinct markets, with no one market or property accounting for more than 21% of ISLE's forecast fiscal 2000 EBITDA."

Guests who visit an Isle resort are not looking for a company that exhibits corporate financial security, they're looking for excitement, entertainment, and an overall good time that includes gambling, shows, food, and extra-curricular activities associated with the locale. These interests are not unusual for any guest at any gaming operation anywhere in the world. What Isle of Capri Casinos, Inc. does to make their guests return is to ensure that the experience is more than the guest anticipated.

> "Enjoyment is not a goal, it is a feeling that accompanies important ongoing activities."
>
> PAUL GOODMAN

The Isle of Capri brand referred to by CIBC is deeply rooted in their philosophy called 'Isle Style,' a Caribbean-based theme that stresses fun. 'Isle Style' is best explained by example.

When I arrived at Isle of Capri Casinos in Biloxi, the door of my car was opened by an enthusiastic employee who smiled and welcomed me with all the southern charm I'd ever imagined. Following check-in, my bags were handled by Don, the bellman, who asked me on the way up to my room how I liked my coffee. Did I like it with cream? With powdered creamer, milk, or real cream? Did I like fluffy towels? Did I prefer a special kind of soap or shampoo? Following his questions and after I was ensconced in my room, Don returned with extra towels and real cream for my coffee. "My goal," he said in answer to my question of why he was doing all this for me, "is to save you a call to housekeeping or the front desk. I don't want you to have to call and ask for anything. I want you to spend your time relaxing and enjoying yourself. It's our 'Isle Style.' I hope you enjoy it."

'Isle Style' attitude is a constant at Isle of Capri Casinos, Inc. And it's not an application, not something learned, it's internal. It's authentic. Capri's training video explains that the company is looking for people who like people, who like to say 'Please,' 'Thank you,' and 'Excuse me;' who like to hold the door open for their guests. In other words, to be a successful Isle of Capri Casino employee you first have to be authentic — job skills can be learned later.

"I think this story explains very well what we're all about," says Robert Boone, Vice President of Human Resources and Risk. "At one time we had a waitress who earned more tips than any of her counterparts but we had to let her go because our guests and her coworkers constantly complained about her attitude. This was supported by the poor satisfaction scores she received from the guests. She was earning more money because she hustled. Actually, she worked extremely hard. You wish all employees worked as hard as she did. But she wasn't having fun and she wasn't friendly, and it showed. She was only getting half the picture of what we were looking for. When we told her she was being let go, she didn't understand it. She said she worked harder than anybody. What she was missing was something inside. She didn't like her job, she liked the money; she didn't like the people, she liked efficiency. That's just not 'Isle Style.' I wonder sometimes how much *more* money she'd have made if she had discovered all this and made it part of her."

'Isle Style' is so branded that every employee knows about it, talks about it, believes it, and behaves it. What they talk about is 'being' CAPRI: *"C is for Courteous service. A means*

Attentive — pay attention to your guests and what they'll need before they ask. P is for Playful — have fun and enjoy yourself at work. R is Resourceful and encourages employees to learn new ways to do their job better every day. I stands for Impassioned. Be driven and always strive to be Number One — love your self, love your job, and love Isle of Capri."

It's not 'doing' CAPRI, you notice, it's 'being' CAPRI. 'Being' CAPRI is authentic; it comes from within and is honest. 'Doing' CAPRI is artificial; it's applied and is disingenuous. 'Being CAPRI' is not a marketing slogan, it's a way of life.

'Isle Style' is also more than a marketing theme, it is an operating philosophy that affects Isle of Capri's four constituencies: investors, guests, employees, and local communities. While the effect of 'Isle Style' on guests ultimately affects investors and the worth of the company, it's the effect on the employees that truly makes Isle of Capri Casinos, Inc. the success it has become in less than a decade of existence.

"Our corporate philosophy, which comes directly from our CEO, Bernie," Robert Boone explains, "says 'If you give people more than what they ask for, more than what they need, you will never fall short.' That's why you were given all those towels and the real cream from Don. Yes, that's an expense, and yes, we could save money by eliminating them and you'd never miss them. But once you've experienced that kind of caring and service, you'll talk about it to your friends and it will make you come back. And if you should ever go to another gaming establishment, they will be judged in your mind against the Isle level of service. If they fall short of your expectations, you'll be back with Isle of Capri. That's worth more to us than the few pennies it costs us to provide the extra, unexpected service. Even if you don't use what we provide.

"We believe so much in the value of our employees, and how they think, act, and behave, that in addition to all the training we've already provided and continue to provide, we're entering into a new training initiative called 'Putting People First.' All 11,000 of our employees will participate in this two-day program, which will cost us more than $3.5 million. What's important to us about this initiative is that we don't separate our employees. Staff and management alike participate in the classes. There aren't different level classes for managers and line employees.

"We're a family here and we like to keep people together, not separate them. We will have a key senior manager open and close each session, but otherwise they'll be right in there with the rest of them. And it'll be a fun experience, I'm sure."

Training programs like these are examples of Isle of Capri Casinos's efforts to be conscientious. They try to improve their people, their results, and their level of success. One way that the authenticity of Isle's employees, on all hierarchy levels, is exhibited occurs during their frequent meetings. Quarterly staff meetings, semi-annual manager meetings, and employee of the month awards include skits, songs, presentations, and employees and managers in costumes. Isle resorts are, after all, entertainment complexes and the employees use entertainment in their meetings and presentations. Because it's an authentic behavior, it comes from within; it's not something applied, it's organic. They like to perform.

"That doesn't just happen. We try to hire people who like people, who like to have fun. That's part of our assessment process," Boone continues. "There is an 'Isle Style' personality. It starts at the top with Bernie. This is his second career and he planned it to be fun. When he started to hire key people, he didn't just look in the gaming industry, he looked for people who weren't stuffed shirts, people who had a sense of fun. I came from the Mall of America in Minnesota and my charge here is to do everything we do in an entertaining manner. You can't run an entertainment business in a way that isn't fun and be successful.

"Does it work? Well, look at our people, they love it here. Then, look at our turnover rate. The industry has 60% turnover; ours is only 40%. Most employees in other gaming facilities don't want to go back there after their shift is over. Ours do. And it's not for the gambling because employees aren't allowed to gamble on our property. They come back for the entertainment, the food, and the fun. But mostly they come back because they miss being with their family."

"If you can't have fun while you're working," adds Jack Gallaway, President and CEO, "you're in the wrong job. Find something else. My philosophy is that life isn't a dress rehearsal. You're on stage all the time. This is real. I'm a former General Manager in Las Vegas, Atlantic City, and South Africa. I've also taught Hotel Management and Gaming at the University of Houston. But now, I'm having fun; I'm having a great time at Isle of Capri. I'm one of the last guys from my group who's still working. They're all retired but I'm having too much fun to retire. I'll keep working until I decide I don't want to work any more. Then I'll do volunteer work.

"Isle of Capri Casinos, Inc. is growing rapidly because of our brand and the kind of employees we have. We fight really hard not to lose the fun attitude as we grow. One of the ways we do that is through diversity. We have 30% women and 15% minorities in management. Our staff numbers are higher. We find that choosing to be diverse keeps us fresh and fun.

"One of the interesting, fun things that happened in Tunica, Mississippi turned into an

example of how 'Isle Style' is more than a saying. When we bought the Tunica property, it came with an old fire engine. We asked if they were going to get rid of it and they said it was our problem. Only our people didn't see it as a problem, they saw it as an opportunity. They painted that old fire truck in bright, fun-loving Isle colors, complete with parrots, and drove it around. They used 'Isle Style' and made it a three-dimensional billboard. They parked it in front, they used it for birthday parties, and they drove it in local parades. It worked so well that now every Isle facility has an old fire engine painted 'Isle Style' that *they* use for parades and birthday parties.

"The fire engine is also an example of how Isle tries to standardize. We have the same look, the same restaurants, even the same menu. We want our guests to feel immediately at home no matter which Isle resort they happen to be at. And we want them to feel so comfortable at their favorite Isle resort that they wouldn't hesitate to try another Isle resort, confident that their experience will also be great. Standardization drives a high level of knowledge and confidence through the organization. Each individual can feel free, then, to bring of himself to the daily requirements and interactions of his job, knowing what's expected of him. By having a standardized operating structure, for example, each General Manager of an Isle resort can focus his or her team's energies and creativity on marketing, customer service, product improvement, and cost control. And to making each guest's Isle experience the best it can be."

"My first experience at Isle of Biloxi was memorable," says Kea Bird, Marketing Manager. "I had just been hired out of college and I was in a special group that was being nurtured and developed. We had been given a lot of information and I was new and anxious to do well. So when we were scheduled to go to one of our first meetings, I was feeling pretty limited on time and found myself wishing I didn't have to go. Well, when I got there they whisked us off for a lunch cruise on the Starship. And we just relaxed and talked and got to know each other. Then after lunch, we had the 15 minute meeting I thought I was going to. I was amazed. They made everything so comfortable and seemingly without effort. It was then that I first experienced 'Isle Style.'"

"I was the second person Bernie hired way back in 1990," says Tim Hinkley, Senior Vice President of Operations. "And although I have a food and beverage background and worked at Stouffer's, Schuler's, and Starline, until I came to work for Isle, I'd never even been inside a casino. My focus is to understand the basic needs of both our guests and our employees and to foster loyalty. Loyalty will cause employees to do a good job and guests to come back. We live by our mission statement which says, *'The Mission of Isle of Capri Casinos, Inc. is to be the best gaming entertainment company: Best for its guests, Best for its employees, Best for its communities, Best for its investors. Not the biggest but the best.'*

"We make it a conscious decision to sustain a fun attitude. We provide constant training, frequent communication of information, and regular meetings. And we keep our operating goals fresh. Fun is so important to Isle and its success that it's even part of our operating goals for the year 2000: *1. Grow our team to the next level. 2. Outrun the competition with exceptional guest service. 3. Utilize technology to optimize performance. 4. Have more fun — stay focused. 5. Successfully extend the Isle family.*

"Our semi-annual managers meetings are called Camp Hinksterville. In January, the managers of all our properties get together and we create our operating goals for the next year. In June, we get together again to review the progress. These aren't dry, sterile meetings. We have skits and parodies. And people dress up in costumes and perform. That kind of presentation makes the information more fun and memorable. And it keeps our operating goals fresher in your mind.

"We want to continue to be good at the basics, to keep the small-company, family attitude as we grow. And not to overburden our people with growth because that's not fun. Most of all, we want to continue to keep the right organizational structure — friendly, easy, and accessible. We offer a product that people want. We're trying to create an environment that they want just as much. And we need to have fun while we do it or it won't work."

It's clear from even the most casual interactions that the Isle's employees are both authentic and conscientious. That this is not by chance can be seen in this statement from Isle founder, Bernie Goldstein: "Employee satisfaction translates directly to guest satisfaction. We can't expect our guests to be treated in a first class manner unless the employees are also treated that way."

To achieve its goals, Isle of Capri Casinos, Inc. selects authentic people to become their employees and is conscientious in providing them the tools to succeed.

And to have fun while doing it.

Update: 2006

They talk about it in tones once reserved for Camille, the killer hurricane of 1965. While Camille may have been stronger, Katrina was bigger; and far, far worse.

Like most of America, I sat and watched as this massive hurricane, which fluctuated between a category four and a category five storm, ravaged the Gulf Coast of Mississippi, leaving behind results comparable to the aftermath of war. In Biloxi alone, more than 45,000 homes were destroyed. The downtowns of many south Mississippi cities, towns, and communities were decimated — some flattened level with their concrete slab foundations. Commerce in this historic tourist region was brought to a standstill in the best cases; obliterated in the worst.

Because of my journey to Biloxi and meeting the people of the Isle of Capri Casino, I had a personal interest in what had happened. I had friends who lived in the path of Katrina and I wanted to know if they were alive and well. A week after the storm passed, while much of America was still focused on the drama unfolding in New Orleans, I sent an email to Robert Boone, Vice President of Human Resources at the Isle of Capri in Biloxi asking how he, the employees, and the casino were holding up. His response was immediate and positive: "In general, we're doing okay."

What did okay mean?

Well, consider that The Isle of Capri-Biloxi Casino was a floating barge, per Mississippi law. Consider that it was a total loss. Consider that all 1,200 of its employees were instantly out of work, most of their homes destroyed, all of their homes damaged by the storm.

Consider the story of Rex Yeisley, Isle of Capri Senior VP of Finance. "We had ridden out Hurricane George with no problems. This would be easy, we thought. As the morning wore on, the rain and wind intensified. We watched from a protected alcove on the west side of our house. When the darker clouds passed over, the winds began to circulate like a tornado. As each burst occurred, we could hear shingles tearing off the roof and see them flying with other things that should have been securely attached to someone's house. We also heard a pounding up in the attic.

By the early afternoon, the pounding in the attic had grown louder. My son called me upstairs to his room and we discovered the pounding was the side of the house flapping like a sail against the studs it had pulled away from. I was in the attic trying to find a solution when a wall blew away and exposed the open attic to the wind and the rain . At that moment, it was no longer fun. We all knew the house would suffer a fair amount of damage. We also knew that it was better to stay safe than try to save the house. Being there allowed instant mourning of our loss and at the same time created a bond to keep each other safe."

Yeisley and his family weathered the storm, their home is now rebuilt, and things truly are "okay" for them. The same cannot be said for Doug DeSilvey, a fourteen-year Isle of Capri employee. As he and his in-laws had done for previous hurricanes, they decided to ride out the storm in his in-laws' home. At one point, water started to enter the living room, eighteen feet above the ground. Within hours, Doug, his daughter Donna (also an Isle employee), his ex-wife, and her parents found themselves in an upstairs bedroom looking out at thirty-foot palm trees, covered in raging water. With a loud crack the roof suddenly blew off and came crashing back down at an angle into the bedroom. Water immediately rolled in and rolled everyone out. Doug was separated from the others and wound up in a magnolia tree. Hours later, when the waters began to recede, he was safe. Not so for his daughter, ex-wife, and in-laws whose bodies he saw floating in the receding water.

DeSilvey credits Isle of Capri and its employees for getting him through the aftermath of that experience. Because the company moved so quickly to help its employees and to rebuild the casino, Doug said he was able to focus on others and their problems instead of his grief. He is back at work wearing his daughter's ID card under his own and telling everyone he meets "When you get up in the morning, tell your loved ones how much you love them."

Bill Kessler agreed with DeSilvey on how well Isle took care of its employees during the immediate recovery period. "The Isle did more for my family than FEMA or SBA. I have worked here for ten years and am very proud to be part of the Isle family. After losing everything, the Isle kept me sane and still keeps me that way. The Isle was the only thing normal left in my life. Thank you for the last ten years and hope-fully, at least ten more."

Now consider that The Isle of Capri Hotel, built on land, came through in good shape and was open and in use within a week, housing workers, utility people, employees. It even hosted the state's reconstruction planning meeting.

Consider that the first press release issued by the Isle of Capri indicated that while the extent of the damage was not yet known, the company announced they would pay ALL employees for at least 90 days and salaried employees for six months.

Consider that Isle of Capri Corporate started a Katrina Relief Fund for employees that distributed $2,100,000 to employees to help with recovery costs.

After such considerations, it was apparent that to Robert Boone and the entire staff of Isle of Capri that *okay* meant they were going to make it. That when all was said and done, Isle-Biloxi would be bigger and better than before. That Isle Style had survived.

Certainly, I thought, they *sounded* positive. I wondered if they would be able to pull it off.

I knew Katrina would be the ultimate test of The Isle of Capri's Isle Style philosophy. Team work, authenticity, and fun are a *nice-to-have* when things are going well. The ques-tion was how well would those soft sciences hold up under the stress of catastrophic natural disaster? Would they be there when they were a *need-to-have*?

The answer was that the soft sciences of Isle of Capri not only held up well, they were the most important part of insuring that the casino would not only be rebuilt and be the first to reopen, but also that the company would grow and improve.

To be successful, good companies need their hard sciences to be in good working order. They need a good vision, a good mission, a good action plan, and a good product. Great companies need not only great hard science but also great soft science. That is, they also must have in place a culture that makes work fun. Isle of Capri's Isle Style is more than a set of rules about what employees should say and do in certain situations. Isle Style is a philosophy and a set of behaviors that define and influence how employees think, act, and behave at all times under all situations. For example, one of the first things Robert Boone and his team did was to hold a payday pizza party in the parking lot the Monday after the storm. Not only did the company pay their employees on time, they also told them they would be paid for the next 90 days, whether or not they were able to work. (When it took 120 days to rebuild, they continued to pay them until there were jobs for them.) The party also provided food during a time of stress and allowed team members to connect, share stories, and offer support for each other and for the company as they all began the process of rebuilding.

By December 2005, Isle of Capri-Biloxi Casino was the first of the dozen or so casinos destroyed to be rebuilt and reopened to the public. Isle of Capri President and chief operating officer Tim Hinkley said, "Reopening the Isle-Biloxi marks a major milestone for the state of Mississippi, as well as for our company. This casino was originally the first to open in the market back in 1992 and we are the first land-based Gulf Coast casino to open following the devastation of Hurricane Katrina. Our goal was to put our team members back to work as quickly as possible and I am happy to say that we have succeeded. Our team members are excited to get back to the business of welcoming guests in Isle Style."

Of the 1,200 people employed before the storm, 900 chose to remain in Biloxi to rebuild and to grow with Isle-Biloxi. More than 100 chose to move and work for another Isle of Capri casino. By the fall of 2006, Isle-Biloxi had grown to 1,700 employees, with the vast majority of the new employees coming from the ranks of those who once worked for other casinos that were not yet reopened. Isle Style scored another win when 90% of those new employees chose to remain with Isle of Capri even after their original casinos reopened and offered them back their jobs.

One such employee was Melanie Pankonin. "I worked at the Grand Casino Biloxi for six years before Katrina. After the storm, the Grand wasn't open and I was able to get a job as a Guest Service Representative at Isle-Biloxi. When the Grand reopened, I decided to stay on at Isle. I love this job and the people I work with. Management treats me like a team member and not a number and that's important to me. They care about me and they value my opinion."

Brian Casey agrees with Melanie. "Everyone in Biloxi knows that the Isle stood by its people during and after the storm. I was able to get on with Isle-Biloxi as a manager and they've given me the opportunity to demonstrate my abilities. I hope to stay here for a long time."

There were four external factors which allowed Isle-Biloxi to reopen quickly.

1. Isle of Capri's insurance was so good that payments covered their damages within two percent.
2. Because Isle-Biloxi was in the midst of an expansion project when Katrina hit, they had already ordered all new slot machines that had yet to be delivered. This allowed Isle-Biloxi to have nearly instant access to the mechanical heart of their gaming operation — slot machines — once the new structure was completed.
3. It was clear to everyone, including the Mississippi legislature, that the state law requir-

ing casinos to be built floating on water was the cause of huge amounts of unnecessary damage and expense. The Grand Casino, for example, which had also essentially been built on a barge, was ripped from its moorings and pushed 1000 yards inland. (The structure had to be cut into quarters and hauled away for demolition.) Seeing the result of their original well-intentioned but impractical regulations, the legislature quickly passed a new law that allowed for the construction of on-land casinos. Without this, it is unlikely that many casinos, if any, would have been rebuilt. Since casinos supply the second-highest level of income, taxes, and financial return to the area, gaming's wishes were seriously and speedily considered.

4. Mississippi came to a political action plan faster than did neighboring Louisiana. Within days of the storm's first impact, Mississippi governor Haley Barbour put together a commission to jump-start rebuilding and asked Netscape founder Jim Barksdale to be chairman. Barksdale funded the commission with $1,000,000 of his own money and encouraged the Knight Foundation to match it. As of fall 2006, New Orleans had *no* plan for demolition, clean-up, or reconstruction.

While their hard sciences were excellent, their planning was top-notch, and they were fortunate in having instant access to replacement slot machines, there is no question that it was the strength of their soft sciences that allowed Isle-Biloxi to recover as quickly as it did from the ravages of Katrina. Not only were they the first casino to reopen, but when they rebuilt they expanded. Now, Isle of Capris-Biloxi plans to build a *second* casino on the Mississippi Gulf Coast.

Hurricane Katrina was a natural disaster on a scale which had not been seen in this country in our lifetime. While it may take decades for the entire region to recover fully from the effects of the storm, the culture of Isle Style has allowed Isle-Biloxi to withstand the worst possible outcome: closing up shop, moving away, and taking 1,700 jobs with them.

Katrina was also a test of the authenticity of the members of the Isle-Biloxi team. It is not unusual to get good performance from companies and individuals in good times. It's what happens in hard times that matters. If relationships are strong and people truly authentic, it will be obvious in both good times and bad.

When a company's culture does not support or invest in its employees, then what those employees do in hard times will be uncertain. If, however, a company has a robust foundation of trust, respect, and loyalty, and has learned to laugh and love together, that company will be able to weather any storm.

Even a storm called Katrina.

■

The Balance Key

BEFORE YOU CAN BE AUTHENTIC, YOU HAVE TO BE IN BALANCE. The ability to keep all your pie pans spinning is a real challenge in a world that moves at the speed of light. If you are not in balance, however, you cannot be the authentic you.

Balance is the conscious effort to choose what you put on your plate, to select the right complement of activities that will combine to produce a desired outcome. It is the ability to keep both the big picture and the details in focus at the same time. Balance is the flexibility to change a plan and seize the spontaneous moment that promises to enhance your intended result.

One of the secrets to a balanced life is to not live by an all-or-nothing mentality — seek moderation. That doesn't mean you can't be passionate about some things. You can. And you should be. It means, rather, that you need to add other elements to your mix so that one side of your life doesn't dominate every waking moment.

Balance also requires that you don't let one thing go untended until it is out of control, or that you don't try to do too much at the same time. In either case, you will eventually be overwhelmed and find yourself out of balance.

Life is neither a diet nor an orgy; life is an ongoing buffet line from which you should choose only what you need at the moment, in the full confidence that when you need more, it will be there for you.

When you are used to living in balance, you will notice when your world begins to tilt precariously in one direction, and take the necessary steps to readjust it and return to a state of balance, rather than try to muscle the outcome through sheer dint of will alone. Restoring balance requires change, not strength.

In order for you to be your authentic self, your life must be in balance.

■

To every thing there is a season, and a time to every purpose under the heaven;

A time to be born, and a time to die; a time to plant, and a time to pluck up that which is planted;

A time to kill, and a time to heal; a time to break down, and a time to build up;

A time to weep, and a time to laugh; a time to mourn, and a time to dance;

A time to cast away stones, and a time to gather stones together; a time to embrace, and a time to refrain from embracing;

A time to get, and a time to lose; a time to keep, and a time to cast away;

A time to rend, and a time to sew; a time to keep silence, and a time to speak;

A time to love, and a time to hate; a time of war, and a time of peace.

ECCLESIASTES 3:1

PRINCIPLE EIGHT
Be Choiceful

EMBRACE THE WHOLE PERSON

To be choiceful means to *give yourself* permission — permission to perform, permission to choose how you will behave, permission to be your full fun self. The only thing in life we have power over is our self; it's the only thing we can change. Being choiceful means we decide who we will be and how we will act, it means we have the permission to become. To be choiceful means to take the world in your own hands; it is the ultimate empowerment.

Being choiceful does not require extra money, time, or energy. It is simply a matter of deciding. It is a conscious decision.

True fun is the result of making good choices; it is not something you choose to do, it is something you choose to become. When you choose fun, you choose to bring the best of yourself to work each day.

If you find yourself lost and work is no longer fun, be choiceful. To be choiceful is to be proactive — create the world in which you choose to live.

To feel inspired, be choiceful.

■

"Happiness is not a matter of good fortune or worldly possessions. It is a mental attitude. It comes from appreciating what we have, instead of being miserable about what we don't have. It is so simple, yet so hard for the human mind to comprehend."

Russell-Rogat acquired by
Lee Hecht Harrison

When I need information, I have a lot of choices. I can go to the library, I can use the Internet, or I can go to breakfast with a friend. My favorite choice, of course, is the one that combines information with social interaction and food — breakfast.

Which is how I came to be with Jane Russell and Rita Jaessing Brauneck, both of Russell-Rogat, an outplacement firm in Cleveland, Ohio. We were discussing, among other things, *Fun Works* and my search for case companies to illustrate the principles of Fun/Work Fusion. When I mentioned that I was looking for a company to represent the Fun Works living laboratory of Be Choiceful, Jane looked at Rita and then at me and suggested that I listen to *her* story because she might just have a company I could include in the book — hers. I listened and she was right.

Jane's story dealt with the buzzwords of the last quarter century — downsizing, rightsizing, and merger. But what was of the greatest interest to me was that although she dealt daily with the potentially depressing subject of people who have recently lost their jobs due to downsizing, Jane's business values stressed behaving in a positive, respectful manner that emphasized fun.

Russell-Rogat began in 1984 when GE Lighting, to facilitate the two-year closing of one of their plants, hired Jane Russell who was then running support groups for the unemployed at a YWCA. "This was a big project," Jane recalled, "so I recruited Amy Rogat and Amy Schuster to help me out. During the next two years, we began to formalize our company philosophy as we helped the GE employees work through their transition.

"1984 was during the infancy of the outplacement industry and we decided that if our work ever ceased to be fun, that we were 'out of here.'

> "I know what happiness is
> for I have done good work."
>
> ROBERT LOUIS STEVENSON

Fun became a primary value of how we were going to do business. There was enough stress involved with clients who were in the process of losing their jobs that we just knew we couldn't add to the problem by being sad, low-key, or unenthusiastic. So we made it a point to be fun, to have fun. We told jokes, we laughed, and we looked forward to the new day.

"Our company motto, 'From Beginning to Beginning,' came out of those days. We were tremendously influenced by William Bridges' theories of transition — 'you can't begin anything new unless you bring closure to the old.' And that became our working philosophy. We stress bringing closure before the individual goes on. If there's still unfinished business, it's not possible to take your best self to your new position. Closure is a choice, certainly, but it's a choice we feel must be made if your future is going to become what you envision.

"So, we end each transition with a celebration. Our goal is to make each transition respectful and fun. We help our outplaced clientele learn to make their transitions in a positive, choiceful way, and learn to have fun while managing tough decisions. Our reward in this process is seeing individuals who come in angry, uncertain, or confused and leave confident in their future. We help them go from one of the low points in their lives to a high point. And for us, that's the joy of what we do.

"The outplaced find themselves in the position they're in without any choice on their part. We stress to them that getting out of that position successfully, however, is *totally* their choice. That what happens next is up to them. Even when life is *not* our choice, it's *still* our choice what happens next."

In 1986, following their initial project success with GE, Jane Russell and Amy Rogat incorporated as Russell-Rogat, hired Amy Schuster as their first employee, and opened their first office. That space was so small that when their first post-GE client entered the office for his initial visit, Jane had to stand behind the door so that the client could enter. Amidst much laughter about their ridiculously small office and the maneuvering required to get around in it, the client offered them a contract because of their expertise but suggested that for ease of meeting next time, they might consider renting a larger space. Because of Russell-Rogat's ability to laugh at their problems, that client remains a client today and their small-office story is one they continue to tell with much affection. Today's offices now take up nearly a whole floor in a modern office building and are designed to make people feel comfortable.

"The second thing we incorporated into our philosophy," Jane continued, "was that 'Family Comes First.' And that applies both to our company and to our outplaced clients, whom we call candidates. Our offices, by choice, are comfortable, not marble. We want our clients to *want* to come here, to feel at ease, to feel like we're their family. We know that job loss is felt as much by a candidate's family as by the candidate themselves, so we welcome children and spouses. And when we celebrate, we celebrate as family, not as individuals.

"When one of our candidates leaves our group for new employment, we celebrate that transition with a bagel party. Those of us remaining celebrate the success along with the newly employed. We could choose to do nothing or we could choose to celebrate. Celebration is a perfect way to bring closure; it's an excellent choice."

When Amy Rogat retired in the beginning of 2000, the staff celebrated that transition in the same manner they celebrate transitions with their candidates — they threw a party. And to commemorate Amy's retirement, they created a video called *Where's Amy?* Various members of the staff acted like roving reporters conducting on-location interviews with other staff members in a humorous recounting of Amy's various habits, discovering in the process that Amy was no longer going to be found at Russell-Rogat.

When Jane celebrated her 60th birthday with a much-deserved vacation, the staff produced a photo album called *While the Cat's Away…* containing pictures of forthcoming revelry, skylarking, and general goofing-off! Jane laughed, the staff laughed, and Jane still took her vacation knowing full well that because the mice were free to choose anything they wanted, they would choose to help their candidates succeed before they would choose to  goof off, despite what their fanciful photo album suggested!

"This is really a family," Amy Schuster says. "Family transcends everything else. It's how we think; it's how we behave. And we have fun. There's always laughter in this office. That makes it fun to work here.

"I don't ever get up in the morning and think, 'Gee, I don't want to go to work today.' I love my job and I love the people I work with. The family feeling allows us to be ourselves. People here see the good in you and make you believe in yourself; they pull at your strings so that you can be the best you can be. And we treat our clients in the very same way, like family. We're happy for them when they find new employment. Our celebrations when they leave are honest; we really *are* happy."

"When I came here as a candidate," Senior Vice President/General Manager Rita Jaessing Brauneck recalled, "I wanted to continue making a difference in my work. Unbeknownst to me, Jane and Amy were looking for a partner so that they could create a succession plan. I liked what I'd experienced here and I liked the values of this company. So when they asked me if I would be interested in becoming their partner, I said *yes*! Yes, because Russell-Rogat was different! I knew I wanted to work where people care and where people count; where family came first, where it was fun to be everyday, and where I could wear any one of my crazy hats and no one would notice!"

Greg Reynolds, Vice President Business Development, says, "It's assumed that the work we do, outplacement, is doom and gloom. But it doesn't have to be. We practice the Golden Rule and we tease a lot. Having fun kind of puts things in perspective. If you can't laugh at yourself and your situation, you can't grow beyond it. What makes it fun is that I can depend on everyone. We have low politics and high investment and involvement in all decisions. Our goal for our candidates is to help them manage transitions in a joyful way. It's their choice, we want them to make the choices that will help them reach their goals."

One of Russell-Rogat's earliest challenges as a new company concerned a Mexican bank transition — 10,000 employees to be outplaced and six career centers to be created throughout Mexico. Initially, Jane and Amy refused the contract because they weren't sure they were ready to take on something that huge, especially considering the inherent language difficulties. The bank hired another company but quickly terminated the arrangement and returned to Russell-Rogat, begging them to take the project. "Reluctantly," Jane recalled, "we agreed. Fortunately for us, Karen Saum, one of the members of our staff team, spoke Spanish fluently. Still, it was a real struggle and quite difficult; but we finished and the bank was thrilled. We learned several things. One, we needed to charge more, and two, we needed to transfer the business leadership to the person who spoke Spanish. We did both and Karen Saum became the president of the International Division."

In 1998, they approached the Panama Canal Commission about Russell-Rogat providing retirement planning to American employees affected by the transition of the Panama Canal. The Commission agreed. On January 1, 2000, the 256 remaining American families were without jobs. Some of them sought work in Panama, but most wanted to return to the United States. While most of the candidates were Americans by birth, many had not lived in the States in years; many of their children had *never* lived here. In addition to dealing with individual candidates, Russell-Rogat facilitated a linkage to alumni networks of Panama Canal employees to make the transition easier once the families returned to the States.

Success stories like these put a national spotlight on Russell-Rogat; with it came the attention of suitors seeking acquisition by merger.

"In 1999," Jane continued, "we were approached by Lee Hecht Harrison, one of the world leaders in career management services. They were interested in acquiring Russell-Rogat into their system. Over the years, we had fielded offers from several outplacement firms. With our international successes, our local reputation with Fortune 500 companies, and our listing in the Weatherhead 100 for two consecutive years, we were a likely prospect and flattered to be asked. Amy and I were on the Board of the Association of Outplacement Consulting Firms International so we were quite familiar with all the players — who they were and what their values were. Until Lee Hecht Harrison came along, we had not found a company whose values were so similar. Family and fun were high on their list, too.

"The merger and the transition were handled in the same way we handle all our business dealings — with fun and laughter. Even the due diligence, which can be daunting and off-putting, was fun. Everyone enjoyed the process and the people involved liked each other. We knew then that we were a match.

"My philosophy," Steve Harrison, President of Lee Hecht Harrison, told me, "is that there's more to life than work. That's the philosophy we bring to our outplaced clientele and that's the philosophy we bring to our acquisitions. Before we look at a company's bottom line, we look at their character. Russell-Rogat had the character and philosophy we needed

> "A master at the art of living draws no sharp distinction between his work and his play; his mind and his body; his education and his recreation.
>
> "He hardly knows which is which, he simply pursues his vision of excellence through whatever he is doing and leaves others to determine whether he is working or playing.
>
> "To himself, he always seems to be doing both."
> — Supplied by Steve Harrison, Author unknown

first, plus they were profitable. It was a match. I do my best to keep our core philosophy the same today with 144 branches as it was when the company had four offices. I like to think we have the best of both worlds: the economic advantage of a large company and the personal touch of a small one."

"When I joined Lee Hecht Harrison," Rolf Gruen, Senior Vice President/General Manager, Seattle told me, "I had just been laid off after nine years of working with a humorless organization. When they said I was gone, I said, 'Thank you.' I made the commitment to myself to use my innate gift of humor in whatever I did and never again to mute it like I had for nearly a decade.

"This is a business that delivers difficult news and I was afraid I'd be limited in my ability to use humor. But I've discovered that delivering difficult news doesn't mean that it's always bad news or that you can't use humor. In fact, it almost requires that humor be an important part of the equation.

"When I was interviewing for the job, I humorously told my interviewer that my family and I only go west over the bridge into Bellview (where the Lee Hecht Harrison offices are located) twice a year so I'd need something good to convince me to change that. As the interviewing process progressed, I'd send postcards with things like, '...crossing the bridge was fun today...' and '...had a lovely view coming west....' I wasn't sure if my humor was going to help or hurt my chances to get hired, but I had chosen to live a life that was true to myself. And humor was part of who I was.

"For the last interview I baked a cake and carried it in my briefcase so that we could celebrate if I got hired. They must have liked the real me because I got hired; but I chickened out and brought the cake home, untouched. So, for my first day at work, I baked another cake and we celebrated!

"My most famous stunt was the gift I gave the General Managers at the 25th Anniversary Party in 1999. I had been joking that Steve Harrison, one of the founders, had made sure we had every conceivable type of clothing with Lee Hecht Harrison on it but boxer shorts. So I hunted down a company that could do that and brought monogrammed shorts to the meeting. I was a little concerned at first that I was entering into a career-limiting stunt but I decided that this was who I was and how I wanted to live, so I went ahead with it.

"The first person to come up and congratulate me was Steve. He said we need to remember to have fun and he wanted a pair for himself.

"What this proves to me is that I have a choice in how I want my work life to be and it's up to me to make the right choices: where I work, who I work with, and how I behave. It's my choice to make work fun or not. I believe work has to be fun. If you're not enjoying your work, then it isn't play; work has to be play and play is good. Good work is when you truly are being who you are."

"Lee Hecht Harrison shows the value they place on individualism," states Beth Sweeney, VP of Business Development Cleveland, Ohio. "They give you the freedom to develop your role, the choice to rise to the occasion, and the confidence to be trusted. This is my opportunity for self-direction; it's my choice to seize that opportunity and apply myself. We give our candidates the tools to make choices, too. We help them see all the opportunities they have, and help them make choices."

Greg Reynolds concurred. "We encourage them to look at being outplaced as if they've been given the gift of time. For the moment, they have time and resources to discover and to do things they've always wanted to do but haven't been able. With their newly found time, our candidates have done everything from hot air balloon rides to going to morning mass every day for a month. Once they start to make choices in their life like that, it becomes easier to make career choices. We support the resiliency of the human spirit and we celebrate when they seize the opportunities and leave us for new careers."

China Gorman, Lee Hecht Harrison's Chief Operating Officer reflects: "I left a competing company after nine years when I experienced a culture crisis — our values simply didn't match. Like Lee Hecht Harrison, I value quality, integrity, respect, and fun. My fun comes from the knowledge that I am helping people in a balanced way. We are intense about business, skills, and placement; and we have fun to relieve the stress. Even within our organization, we create scenarios for our General Managers at their annual meeting that focus on fun. We plan unstructured time and just be together. When we engage the heart, the real fun occurs.

"When they walk into a Lee Hecht Harrison office, our clients, candidates, and visitors feel that this is a place of support. Not just the warm and fuzzy kind of support, but a support that has a strong structure and a clear direction. They can tell this is a safe, supportive, confidential place to be. To maintain this atmosphere, we select our employees very carefully. Our employees are the heart of our success. They are responsible for extending understanding, empathy, and support to our candidates — support that maintains a balance between serious and fun. The kinds of employees who make Lee Hecht Harrison successful are the ones who want to make a positive choice about their contributions each day. This is a very competitive and serious business, but it has to be fun to be successful."

"I don't think you can legislate fun," Steve Harrison adds. "You need to find people who have a great sense of humor. It has to be part of them. The notion of fun is a serious game. We're in the business of transferring strength — from our employees to our candidates. It's our job, through seriousness and humor, to strengthen depleted individuals.

"I believe we have a disarmingly open culture. We have an intranet that bonds people like Velcro®. It's a virtual water cooler around which people share information, exchange greetings, and have fun. We celebrate everything."

"We don't celebrate that people have lost their jobs," says Rolf Gruen, "but we make the situation fun by encouraging our candidates to bring the full sense of their humanity to the situation, and that means humor, too. Choice is embracing the whole person. And the whole person includes fun, even at work."

"By trying not to take life too seriously," Steve Harrison adds, "we engage everyone in the process and make our choices pleasurable."

So, how did Jane Russell feel about Russell-Rogat being acquired? Was her choice pleasurable? "Lee Hecht Harrison treats each of its 160 offices worldwide as if it were an independent company, which enables us to conduct ourselves in virtually the same manner as when we were Russell-Rogat. We are free to be our full, fun selves. Our culture hasn't changed much at all. Lee Hecht Harrison supports us totally and gives us full authority and responsibility to succeed.

"It's been a very good choice for us."

Life is a series of choices. Be choiceful. It's fun.

■

Update: 2006

My relationship with Jane Russell and Amy Rogat goes back twenty years to our first days in business, theirs as co-founders of Russell-Rogat and mine as the founder, president, and janitorial engineer for Catalyst Consulting Group. In the nearly seven years since Jane, Rita Brauneck, and I had that breakfast meeting and decided that Russell-Rogat would be the Fun Works living laboratory for Be Choiceful, and in the six years since they were acquired by Lee Hecht Harrison, I have maintained my friendship with both women.

While both Jane and Amy have since retired, I remain strongly connected to Rita. Last year, our two companies co-hosted a presentation by Harvey MacKay based on his book *We Got Fired*. We each invited clients and, as always, everyone had a good time and a great experience.

Because of my continuing relationship with Rita, I have kept tabs on Lee Hecht Harrison's Cleveland office. I knew that it continued to grow, that it was the leader in outplacement in the market, and that Lee Hecht Harrison's corporate headquarters was pleased with its acquisition and pleased with the value being added to the national organization.

"In 2004, we moved our offices," Rita said. "We worked with our architect and designer to create a space that would make our guests feel welcome, especially our job seekers. What we have is very colorful and filled with whimsical art. Everyone can tell the minute they walk in that this is a place they'd like to be.

"Do we still have fun?" Rita continued. "Well as part of our process of 'onboarding' a staff member, we recently closed the office for a drumming session with a local expert. We all simultaneously felt good and silly as we drummed away, using different beats in different tempos. It was a unique experience and there was lots of laughter. So, yes, we still have fun."

And they still maintain their culture of fun and caring. A small, but telling example is the *Make A Difference* portion of each staff meeting during which any staff member may tell a story about a colleague who has made a difference, for a candidate, customer, or another staff member. These are brief but immediate acknowledgments of thanks that help to retain and maintain the cultural roots of Russell-Rogat and Lee Hecht Harrison.

As a result of deciding to include Russell-Rogat in *Fun Works*, I met and became friends with Rolf Gruen, Senior Vice President and General Manager, Lee Hecht Harrison Seattle. Over the last six years, I have found myself frequently in Seattle, researching books and articles, and consulting. Each time I visit, I connect with Rolf for dinner or coffee or a visit to Pike Place Fish, the Fun Works living laboratory for Give Permission to Perform. During these meetings we trade stories, trade books, and talk about our respective businesses.

From Rolf I have learned that Lee Hecht Harrison is still the fun place to work it was when he first joined and he and I first met. Rolf is still the kind of guy who makes all those around him enjoy his presence.

"Several years ago," Rolf said, by way of explaining that he still had fun, "I took stickers of a starfish (an internal corporate symbol that represents how we assist our clients) to the annual international leadership convention. I put them on the name tag of everyone I talked to and kept track of who and how many people I managed to meet that year. As you can imagine, many folks gave me a weird look when I stuck my starfish on their name tag. However, the next year, I was surprised when people started coming up to me and asked to get *stuck*. Needless to say, I met a lot more people that year. And the next, and the next. People actually look forward now to saying hello each year and getting stuck. It's fun and it connects all us very strongly."

But Rolf is more than just a soft-science maven; Rolf is the consummate businessman. As such, he is a large part of the reason that Lee Hecht Harrison has turned its hard science advantages into long-term rewards for its clients and financial success for the company.

"Lee Hecht Harrison made the choice a few years ago," Rolf told me, "to not only be the leader in outplacement services but to react to the growing economy and expand into coaching and other employee-retention services and activities. Our focus is no longer limited to downsizing and job loss. Because of the choices we made, our services now include the skills and training to keep and retain good people. Our services now cover the entire life cycle of a career."

This change of focus also impacts Rita and the Cleveland office. "Organizations rarely face just downsizing. They now reinvent themselves to redistribute work," Rita says. "There is ongoing attention inside organizations to having the right people in the right places and to moving work where it can be done effectively. Now, we're there to help them do just that.

"We are also focusing on developing further our own leadership tools using our *Coaching Practices for Leaders*, a developmental process for shifting our culture toward one that values coaching. It's the business equivalent of insuring that the cobbler's children have good shoes!"

To help maintain their focus and continued success, Lee Hecht Harrison follows these four guiding principles:

1. **Commit to the highest degree of professional and ethical behavior.**
2. **Create extraordinary experiences at every opportunity.**
3. **Reward achievement and initiative, and hold each other accountable for results at all levels.**

4. **Respect one another as partners who bring talent, intelligence, and compassion to our work.**
* **In addition, Lee Hecht Harrison continues to follow a fifth, unwritten, principle: Be Choiceful.**

Lee Hecht Harrison made the choice to support the United States Winter Olympic Games by supporting the athletes not only during the games but between them and beyond. They partnered with the U.S. Olympic Committee to create The Athlete Career Program. This career management program is a comprehensive initiative that provides career education, professional development, and job opportunities. Because the finish line is only the beginning, The Athlete Career Program was developed to help athletes earn an income while in training, develop a resume that effectively conveys the value of their unique backgrounds, and gain meaningful work experience after their Olympic Games.

As a result of the choices Lee Hecht Harrison makes, they have received honors and awards that support their choices. These are a few:

* **2006 – Women in Business Achievement Award, Paulette Ashlin, Senior Vice President and Managing Director, North Carolina Operations**
* **2006 –** *Leadership Excellence* **Top 100 Leadership Development Company**
* **2005 – Alfred P. Sloan Award for Business Excellence in Workplace Flexibility, Dallas Office**
* **2006 – Employer All Star Award, Richmond Office**
* **2004 – LHH President's Award for Exceptional Office Performance, Seattle**
* **2003, 2002 – Quality of Excellence Award, Association of Career Management Consulting Firms International.**
* **2003 – LHH President's Award for Exceptional Office Performance, Cleveland**
* **Lee Hecht Harrison also produces awards of its own, naming Brett Wright, St. George Bank, as the Best HR Director, 2004.**

As a result of its powerful hard science and effective soft science working together throughout its entire organization, Lee Hecht Harrison maintains its position as the flagship brand of the Adecco Career Services Division of Adecco, S.A., and generates more than $180 million in annual revenue. Lee Hecht Harrison employs more than 850 people in more than 240 offices in thirty-six countries and is recognized as the global leader in career management and leadership consulting, maximizing organizational success through services that connect people to work, increase effectiveness, and develop superior leaders.

And it does all of this by choice.

■

The Question Key

THE KEY TO BEING CHOICEFUL IS TO ASK QUESTIONS. If we don't question what we've done and what we plan to do, we miss out on the opportunities to improve our results. Your answers to your questions, regardless of what those answers are, will give you choices. Once you have choices, you will have the ability to be choiceful, to create the world in which you live.

To be choiceful, therefore, ask questions.

Here are some questions to get you started:

When was the last time I laughed?

Am I having fun at work every day?

What are my recent successes?

What could I do to improve them?

What could I do to make them better?

Am I feeling disconnected from my work and my working relationships?

Why do I think this is happening?

What could I do to change that?

What are my long-term goals for my business?

What are my long-term goals for my personal life?

How would I describe my current level of success on a 1-to-10 scale?

If I could do one thing to improve my life immediately, what would it be?

If I know that the only thing keeping me from bringing my whole, fun self to my work is my fear, why haven't I addressed that?

■

"People are always good company
when they are doing
what they really enjoy."

SAMUEL BUTLER

PRINCIPLE NINE
Hire Good People and Get Out of Their Way

TRUST YOUR EMPLOYEES TO USE THEIR JUDGMENT

If we have hired well and we trust our employees with the most valuable assets of the organization, then why not trust their judgment on how to use their full fun selves to achieve company objectives?

Some people fear that if they give permission for fun, employees will take advantage of the situation and shift the focus from work to fun. This is only a risk if we approach fun as a reward for working versus being part of the work. If our mental model is work hard first and have fun later, we may create a dynamic that contributes to individuals feeling like they are on a low-fun diet. And diets, as we are all aware, often result in bingeing. When fun is 'in' the work and results from the satisfaction of good work and good working relationships, then there is little risk of 'when the cat's away the mice will play.'

When the work is both worthwhile and fun, then valuable employees will want to stay; where there is a committed, energized, productive group of employees, others will want to join. The integration of fun with work creates a natural-attraction force that is irresistible to good people.

Discover the secret to success: Hire good people and get out of their way.

■

Lou Harris & Associates
recently asked more than
1,000 'peak performers'
what kind of workplace they
would be reluctant to leave.
74% responded: "One that
promotes fun and closer work
relationships with colleagues."

One Prudential Exchange
Safe to Say

Newark, New Jersey, is an aging American city on its way back up. My two trips through it by car showed me that its bleak, hard times, which I had heard about for years, were being shaken off and a new growth was emerging — a perfect metaphor for my next Fun Works living laboratory, the One Prudential Exchange Team (OPX).

OPX occupies space within the Leadership & Learning Department on the sixth floor of the Prudential headquarters building in downtown Newark. Prudential and its massive headquarters could easily find a home in the downtown skyline of neighboring giant, New York City. Yet the company remains as faithful to and supportive of the community of Newark as it is to its employees.

Established in 1875, Prudential has revenues of more than $26 billion and, in the past, has displayed some characteristics of a classic McGregor Theory X corporation — hierarchical decision making concentrated at the top of the organization and a high aversion to risk. Since Chairman and CEO Art Ryan took the helm in 1994, and through the efforts of OPX, the company has made significant strides to evolve into a more effective Theory Y organization. Today, more individuals in the company embrace a process orientation, a desire to enlist the talents of all people, high trust in the individual, and the creation of an intellectually safe environment.

America's recent and rapid love for investing has changed more than the daily average of the Dow, it has changed the very way in which companies think about who they are, what they do, and who they serve. Companies that compete most favorably on the stock exchange must adapt to the marketplace, and respond to the needs and desires of their owners — their stockholders. Companies that are mutually owned by policyholders, like Prudential, have less pressure on them to succeed and tend not to develop strong performance-oriented cultures. When Ryan took the reins in 1994, he recognized that the company was in need of change, drastic change. One response to that need was the formation in 1997 of the concept called One Prudential Exchange, OPX.

The OPX team was charged with the responsibility to help create a new culture for the company and spread the message throughout its 60,000 employees quickly and effectively. OPX's roster consisted of a blend of outside facilitators and Prudential employees. "The secret to our success," says Vice President Jody Doele, "is actually the secret to the success of any organization — hire the right people. I believe the right person has the right values, a sense of passion for their work, and a willingness to build a good work community. The corporate culture in America is shifting from the 'good soldier' to a working community. The goal, when you put together a group of people, is to create a team with a culture of trust, confidence, and vulnerability. You also have to create an environment in which they feel safe to make choices."

"In our team, we have what we call a 'safe to say' environment," adds OPX Team Leader Kimberley Christine. "That means that everyone feels confident they won't be penalized for anything they say. In the 'old Prudential' culture, saying the wrong thing could be detrimental to your career. In the OPX team, we have the latitude to pursue our work with passion. We embrace mistakes as an opportunity to learn. But you have to be open and honest about mistakes or it doesn't work."

"I require two things from the people I hire," Jody continues. "One, they must believe they can effect change and make a difference; and two, they must want to grow personally. The work of OPX is monumental both in its creation and the scope of its effect. We need people who believe in that and want to be part of it."

"OPX is a huge undertaking," says Susan Sustana, Associate Manager. "Our goal was to make a big undertaking bearable and not to become consumed by the process. We came together as a group doing things that fostered an environment of camaraderie, both in the workplace and after hours. We made it fun. Fun has to be like that, it just has to happen. It can't be forced, it has to happen naturally. But it needs a positive, safe environment for it to blossom.

"Fun is having passion for your work and linking up with your colleagues. It's hard to have fun by yourself." Susan continues. "The secret is to do something that you love and will enjoy doing. I really care who sits down the hall from me. Able people help to make a great environment and that's when work is fun. Work is fun for me because I work with really talented people. I find a little piece of me in every person with whom I work. We are all idealists and realists at the same time. We have a lot of latitude."

> "I never did a day's work
> in my life. It was all fun."
>
> ## THOMAS ALVA EDISON

Rachael Elwork, the newest member of the OPX team, recalls, "On the team you can get involved in anything you are interested in, you just have to have the passion for it. We could laugh all day, even through the hardest times. There is a real balance between stress and relaxing. I think that's because the team is filled with people with exceptional qualities and drive. We bring our passions to the work and we develop deep relationships with other team members. It's all about people. Fun is energy; it's the commitment to each other and the project; it's the belief in the work and the creation of work relationships that become friendships."

"The secret to the success of the OPX team," explains Sharon Wright, Director of Human Resources in Scranton, Pennsylvania, "was the fairly rigorous selection process of the team. They looked for people who were open, who were willing to learn from others and from their own mistakes, and for people who had a common attraction to this kind of work. It was fun because it was safe, there wasn't any competition amongst us to use the process to get ahead or take advantage of anyone, we were allowed to fail, and there was lots of humor and warmth."

What was the goal of OPX? OPX was an exercise through which all 60,000 of Prudential's employees learned about the external world in which Prudential operates, its strategies to survive and grow, how it makes money, and what the company needs to do to move forward. The OPX team came to the agreement that instead of having this information disseminated via memo or newsletter, via lecture or video, the information would cascade down from top to bottom and that the ultimate learning experience would be a series of more than 200 meetings nationwide in which *each and every* employee would participate using a tool called a Learning Map®. The goal was to create 100% participation and 100% involvement. Senior managers taught managers; and managers in turn taught their employees. Everyone had a role and an opportunity to participate. And everyone learned more about Prudential than they thought was possible. The OPX sessions, the result of years of thinking and planning, worked. They worked so well they were written up in dozens of publications from *EIU Strategic Finance* to *Human Resource Executive.*

Just thinking about the logistics of *scheduling* 60,000 employees is mind-boggling. Imagine the preparations that had to be made regarding location, food, staffing, overnight accommodations and so forth. That's where the 18 years of meeting-planning expertise of Debbie Boschee, CMP, became invaluable for the success of OPX.

"Before we could even begin to worry about food and beverage, audio-visual equipment, invitations, materials, site supervision and location," Debbie said, "we had to discover where our employees lived so we could make intelligent decisions about where we should hold these meetings. You have no idea how long something like that can take. But I really enjoyed it, especially because I knew the results of my efforts were going to impact this company in a favorable way.

"During my first 20 years in Prudential, I could sense that our environment made it difficult for people to make a decision, to take a chance. People were afraid to make a mistake, to fail. Since I've been involved with One Prudential Exchange, I can see that the growth, energy, and fun we created are beginning to spread. Working in my division now is almost like working in a different company! The messages of OPX support an environment of open communication and the willingness to confront each other and support one another. Prudential is working to create a new company culture and I can see the results already.

"We work really hard but we also take the time for celebration and down time. We take pictures, we go to weddings and birthdays as a team, and we have barbecues. It's the people who make up the unit who make it so much fun. But it's also our supervisors.

"Jody is a great leader. She trusts us. She lets us do what we're supposed to do — be creative and solve problems. I have grown and learned from her. Our whole department is based on teamwork. We will drop anything to help someone out. We have great peer-to-peer recognition. If you do something good, everyone lets you know in no uncertain terms. We are coworkers, but we have become friends."

Which leads me to Wilma and Janine, coworkers who worked down the hall from each other, sat in the same meetings for years, and knew each other but not well. Not until their mutual experience working on a large-scale reorganization, that is. Now they are such a pair that they often finish each other's sentences. When they are together, laughter is not far away. They exude energy, confidence, and comradeship. "This is the most awesome jambalaya," exclaims Wilma Harris, Director of Human Relations, Newark, referring to how well One Prudential Exchange worked. "Just like in jambalaya, you've got to have good ingredients. But when you put them together, blend them, and let the flavors work together, you get a final product that's better than the individual pieces."

When your work is a tasty meal like that, what hunger do you create? The hunger for more work!

"I never thought I would miss a meeting like I miss the OPX meetings now that the national roll-out is complete and we've had our final debriefing," says Janine Omara, Director of Human Resources, Newark, "but I do. Our work on OPX was engaging. The team wanted to hear what each of us had to say. They were interested in everyone's perspectives. It mattered what you thought. In most business meetings, people don't get passionate about their work. In the competition to prove their individual value, people lose themselves and their humanness. They don't show emotion and they avoid challenging dialogue. The truth often gets lost.

"That's what was different in our OPX meetings. Everyone cared about making it the best it could be and they showed the emotion, the passion, the concern that went along with it. Everyone had a stake in each other's success. I want for you to be good, for us to be good, for Prudential to be vital. There wasn't a sense of competition between employees. We had the synergy of extending our selves and good intentions to each other. Whenever we did anything right, we celebrated our success and we shared the celebration.

"People brought different perspectives to things. We valued and celebrated talent. We could challenge each other. There were no 'Yes-men.' We were a community, open and honest with mistakes. We made a difference in each of our lives and in the workings of the team and ultimately in the lives of everyone who works at Prudential. That was fun. Making a difference in people is fun."

"We got to talking about meetings and things in terms of paprika," Wilma recalls. "Why do you put paprika on deviled eggs? On mashed potatoes? Not for the flavor but just to make them look good! Now when Janine and I are somewhere together and we can tell that what's happening is just to make things look good, we turn to each other and say 'paprika.' We always want to know if we're only functioning at the paprika level. We don't want to function any more at a superficial level, just for show. We want to make a difference."

"Let me tell you a story about our grill man," Wilma says, to which Janine nods her head enthusiastically. "Once we felt how OPX had changed us, we wanted other people to share that feeling, too. There was this new grill man in the cafeteria, but he never smiled, he never looked at you or made eye contact. All he did was scowl and take your order. So Janine and I decided we'd make it our project to bring him out, to let him know he was valuable to us and to himself. For about two months, whether we went to the cafeteria alone or together, we'd say 'good morning' and smile, or ask if he had a good weekend. We'd kid him about overcooking our eggs. Anything to get him to look us in the eye. One time Janine came back and said, 'I got him to smile.' That encouraged us to continue. Eventually, it got to where he would smile and say 'good morning' before we did! He'd even crack a joke. Eventually, our grill man was saying 'good morning' to everyone, not just us. That's the kind of thing that OPX has done for us. It was a great experience."

This wave of One Prudential Exchange will soon be over but its effects on Prudential have just begun. One Prudential Exchange accomplished its goal of creating a compelling message and disseminating it to more than 60,000 Prudential employees across the country in such a way that the culture of Prudential is beginning to change irrevocably, and change for the better. The original goal of making Prudential a more open company, responsive to the needs and desires of the people it serves in the marketplace is proceeding and, from my observations within the Learning & Leadership Development Group, is becoming more and more the norm.

Art Ryan, Chairman and CEO, puts it this way: "OPX is an investment in our people, so that they understand all that is required of the company to be successful in the marketplace. And, importantly, what their role is in the company. I want to see that spirit of winning, that feeling of, 'Yes, there are obstacles, but there are also opportunities; and this company and its people are positioned to win.'"

Because of Ryan's initiative and the sterling results of the execution, Prudential appears to be on that path of winning. Prudential owes its future success in part to One Prudential Exchange and to the dedicated people who were chosen to make it happen.

■

Update: 2006

I first came across Prudential's One Prudential Exchange Program (OPX) through a consultant colleague who was working on the project. He told me "This is a tremendous undertaking, one that should have tremendous results." It sounded like a good idea to me and it fit perfectly into the principle of Hire Good People and Get Out of the Way, so I contacted Prudential.

The project was in the middle of its existence when I started my research and it completed its mission and was scheduled to end by the time the first edition of Fun Works was published. It had accomplished, with spectacular results, its goal of getting 100% of Prudential's employees involved in understanding the workings and goals of the organization. It had achieved its goal of reenergizing the organization's personnel and had started the company on the road to the new beginning that CEO Art Ryan envisioned. Having accomplished its purpose, OPX was retired.

But not for long.

Shortly after being withdrawn from active duty, OPX was brought out of retirement and revived as an on-going, system-wide *learning literacy* tool. And while that's a good thing, the *great* thing is what has happened to Prudential as a result of Art Ryan's initial roll-out of OPX. The *great* thing is that OPX is a near-perfect model for any company that chooses to change its culture. Its action-line is simple: Hire Good People and Get Out of Their Way.

During the last six years, I have followed the changes at Prudential through my own direct research and through that of other colleagues connected to the insurance industry. The positive changes at Prudential in that time are the direct result of the work of OPX and of the good people hired to change its culture. While the world saw and followed the *external* changes at Prudential (the changes in their hard science), those of us who knew about OPX followed the *internal* changes (the changes in the soft science). It was obvious to those who knew of both, that the hard science changes were as successful as they were only because of the wildly successful soft science changes that OPX helped create.

These guiding principles are part of the foundation that supports the soft sciences at Prudential:

- We foster a climate where all associates act with courage, integrity, honesty, and fairness. We are committed to creating an atmosphere that is free of discrimination or harassment of any kind, and where differences are respected and valued.
- We nurture a culture within the Company that is highly moral, making decisions based on doing the right work in the right way for the right results.
- We provide an engaging work environment, where associates can learn, grow and develop, both professionally and personally.

The most impressive of the hard-science improvements at Prudential concern their finances. In the last six years, Prudential has gone through the greatest period of change in its more than 130-year history. The most dramatic change is becoming a publicly owned and traded company.

Prudential (PRU on the New York Stock Exchange) had its Initial Public Offering in December of 2001, three months after 9/11. Even with America's economy at a low ebb as a direct result of the terrorists' sneak attack, Prudential's IPO did well and the company found itself with a significant amount of capital with which to make further changes.

Prudential began to look for initiatives that would improve its revenue generating ability and minimize its negative cash flow. For example, Prudential's property and casualty business generated $2 billion in premiums but lost $1 billion due to Hurricane Andrew all in one year — a huge, damaging loss. Ryan and the management team sold that business and then divested itself of it health-care insurance, mortgage, reinsurance, and credit card businesses. Ryan and the management team also realized that when they could, it would be better to acquire good companies that had the products they needed rather than try to create and develop the products themselves.

The first acquisition they made was of the Japanese Kyoei Life Insurance Company, which they renamed Gibraltar Life. The purchase of Japan's ninth-largest insurer increased Prudential's international business revenue contributions to 40% of the company's earnings and was a significant step in generating new revenue and growth.

Prudential then proceeded to change its business mix by selling divisions and products which did not generate growth-oriented revenues and by adding divisions which would build the company through such things as retirement products and third-party distribution. American Skandia, the Fun Works living laboratory for Celebrate (Principle Eleven), specialized in variables annuities and was a company with a culture that would integrate seamlessly with the newly rejuvenated Prudential. Because American Skandia had been particularly hard hit by 9/11 and had accumulated significant exposures to guaranteed death benefits, Prudential was able to acquire them using their newly generated capital only two weeks before the stock market bottomed out.

In 2003, Prudential bought Cigna's retirement business for 2.1 billion dollars, the largest acquisition in Prudential's history. This purchase added immediately to Prudential's return on equity, as did the purchase of American Skandia.

Shortly after, Prudential merged its securities brokerage with Wachovia Securities and now owns 38% of the third-largest retail broker in America.

Because of its acquisitions and divestments, Prudential now features a business mix superior to that of most of its competitors, with new strengths in retirement, annuities, and international insurance.

Not only has Prudential seen growth and stabilization in its hard sciences, its soft sciences have improved, too. The effect of that improvement can be seen in the more than five pages of awards garnered in the last six years.

Prudential's awards include:

- 2006 — Diversity Inc ranks PRU one of the Top 50 Companies for Diversity for the sixth consecutive year.
- 2006—Human Resources Outsourcing Association names PRU "Relocation Provider of the Year."
- 2005 — National Eagle Leadership Institute confers the CareerFOCUS Eagle Award on Emilio Egea, Human Resources.
- 2004 — Goodwill Home and Mission's Outstanding Corporate Volunteer Service Award.
- 2003 — Star-Ledger ranks Prudential 23rd on the Top 200 Public Companies.
- 2003 — Maryland Work/Life Alliance names PRU an "Excellent Place to Work in Maryland."
- 2003, 2002, 2001 — DiversityInc.com Top 50 Companies for Diversity.
- 2002 — Ebony Magazine recognizes Gabriella Morris as one of Top Foundation Heads in America.
- 2002 — Public Relations Society of America (PRSA) Pyramid Award for "Taking Prudential Public" campaign.
- 2002 — Ranked 6th on Working Woman Magazine Top 25 Companies for Executive Women.
- 2001 — #1 in Milwaukee Journal-Sentinal Analysis for fifteenth year.

Prudential's success can also be seen not only in the awards they receive, but also in the ways they give to the community. Since 1995, Prudential has supported Global Volunteer Day (the first Saturday of October), in which employees are encouraged to give back to the community. Participation in this popular event during the last six years has leaped from 5,000 employees the first year working on 100 projects, to more than 34,000 volunteers in 2005 working on 900 projects in 15 countries. Based on the 2005 hourly value of volunteer time of $17.75, as determined by the Points of Light Foundation, Prudential's employee efforts have exceeded a ten-year cumulative value of more than $20 million.

In 2005, Prudential and its employees responded to the ravages of Katrina by contributing more than $5 million to help Gulf Coast victims with housing assistance, job training, and other daily services.

When Prudential bought CIGNA's retirement business, they kept its headquarters in Hartford, Connecticut, keeping hundreds of families in their homes and in their local communities. In addition, Prudential designated Hartford a "city of interest" which allows the company to focus its financial and charitable contributions on projects of concern to the members of that community, such as the $25,000 it committed to the South Arsenal Neighborhood Development Corporation's Teen Action Center.

When Art Ryan became the first CEO of Prudential to be brough in from outside the Prudential hierarchy, he brought with him a vision of change, a vision that would eventually transform Prudential into a company with more than a half a trillion dollars under management, a company that is a clear leader in the industry, and a company for which people love to work. That transformation can be directly attributed to One Prudential Exchange, OPX.

The secret to the success of OPX is that Prudential searched diligently to find just the right people to be part of this transformational team, people who were willing to stand up and be counted, willing to say what they thought and act on it. Once they had the right team members, Prudential wisely got out of their way and let them work. Not only did this create a working environment in which everyone got along and everyone grew personally, but it created a dynamic in which the output was significantly greater than the sum of its parts.

What Prudential received from OPX was a company transformed from potential stagnation into one leading the way into the twenty-first century, a Fun Works living laboratory for Hiring Good People and Getting Out of Their Way.

■

"To make good metaphors implies an eye for resemblances."

ARISTOTLE

The Metaphors Key

WE LOVE STORIES. WE LOVE TO TELL THEM. We love to read them, to watch them, and to listen to them. We love stories because they help us to understand.

Metaphors are little stories. They are figures of speech; they are words or phrases that suggest similarities. Metaphors help us understand.

A metaphor can take a complex idea and make it simple. A metaphor is a way to communicate simply, memorably, and understandably. When we use metaphors, we can explain and teach more quickly with greater comprehension.

One Prudential Exchange used this metaphor: Our relationship is a dance. As they developed their metaphor more fully, they discovered that, like a dance, it had many elements: Learn the steps, listen to the music, trust yourself and your partner, practice, sometimes you lead, sometimes you follow, don't be afraid to add a spin or a dip, dance with different partners, applaud at the end of a dance, learn a new dance. The work of OPX was hard work, but when they thought of it as a dance, it became fun. And that made their work easier.

Is your work relationship a chain gang? Or is it a circus? Is it a forced march? Or is it a conga line? What metaphor would you use to describe your job? To describe your organization?

Metaphors create mental images so that ideas are easy to remember. When you want to explain your work to new employees, when you want to communicate to them quickly and easily, use a metaphor.

Then stand out of their way.

■

"Respond to every call
that excites your spirit."

RUMI

10

PRINCIPLE TEN
Embrace Expansive Thinking and Risk Taking

LEARN HOW TO HARNESS AND DEVELOP
THE FULL POTENTIAL OF EMPLOYEES

The integration of fun and work requires expansive thinking and risk taking. When we utilize expansive thinking, we learn to 'think beyond the box.' When our thinking expands, we create the room for fun to come into our work. Only then can we embrace the risk of integrating fun and work.

To embrace risk taking means to try new things without fear of criticism, to be able to make mistakes and welcome them as learning, without fear of punishment. To be successful at risk taking, we must overcome our fear of failure; we must be able to bring our whole selves to work without fear of rejection. Once we are successful at expansive thinking, risk taking itself becomes fun.

Nothing great in history was ever accomplished without risk. The risk for great success is the same as the risk for failure — extremely high; the risk involved in producing mediocrity is extremely low. To succeed greatly, we must risk greatly. Risk is inherent in innovation and innovation is the life-blood of our future. Lead the way into the future — don't follow.

Expand your thinking, embrace the risk of fun and work.

■

"There's nothing like a gleam of humor to reassure you that a fellow human being is ticking inside a strange face."

EVA HOFFMAN

Will Vinton Studios
Making Raisins into Stars

When the taxi pulled up to this huge, arching sign proclaiming 'Will Vinton Studios' in Northwest Portland, I have to admit I felt like Dorothy in the Wizard of Oz. After I passed through an overly large door in front of an overly large warehouse-type building, I came to a waiting room where the receptionist greeted me and announced to Will Vinton himself that I had arrived. While I was sitting, waiting to be escorted to his third floor office, I noticed a little wire basket being lowered slowly, from somewhere three floors up, onto the receptionist's desk. The basket was full of mail and I was sure I was in one of Will Vinton's animated short films. This somewhat archaic, yet simple mail delivery system was just the first of many surprises I was to discover in this Fun Works living laboratory of Risk Taking.

You may not know the name, but you surely know the studio's work. Just mention the California Raisins and you're talking about Will Vinton Studios. The M&M's commercials with Steve Baldwin, *The PJs* television series with the voice of Eddie Murphy, the *Gary & Mike* television series, and dozens of shorts and promotions are also Will Vinton Studios projects. Will Vinton Studios, begun in 1976, created, coined, and trademarked an animation process known as Claymation®.

"I was a student of math and science at the University of California at Berkeley," recalls Vinton. "I fell into architecture and that's the degree I graduated with, but I had taken up film making because that's what I was interested in and I started doing short animated films working out of my basement. There was this Spanish architect by the name of Antonio Gaudi who did a lot of work with clay and I was inspired by his work and tried some sculpting myself. Pretty soon I was experimenting with clay and animation and created the process I called Claymation. In 1975 my Claymation® film *Closed Mondays* won an Academy Award®, and that prompted me to start my own company making animated films using clay.

"Today, we're probably the best in the world at creating clay and foam animation. When I first started

the clay animation studio, it was a risk. No one was doing this — and making money at it! Starting my own business was also a risk. If I knew then what I know today about the problems involved in running your own business, I probably wouldn't have started. In fact, I'm *sure* I wouldn't have! But even if it was a risk, it was fun. It was wildly creative for the studio and for me personally. And, it still is.

"Since then we've experimented with dozens and dozens of ways to do animation, some of which we adopted, some have disappeared. This company was founded on experimentation and it's through experimentation that its structure emerges. We always have to be looking at new methods while we perfect the old ones. For example, we're heavily into computer animation processes while we maintain and perfect our traditional animation."

What Will Vinton Studios is all about these day, is the creation of characters — regardless of the medium. Characters like the California Raisins, the M&M's, and the GI Joe-type sports car driver in the Nissan television commercial who rescues the Barbie look-alike from the Ken look-alike in what many advertising authorities claimed was the best television commercial of 1996. Giving inanimate objects human characteristics is not always easy but Will Vinton Studios has taken this risky process and made it an art-form for which they've become famous.

"You have to take risks if you want to create something new and exciting. It's a case of seeing the vision and going for it. You don't always know how you're going to do something when you start, you just know what you want it to look like and you work to achieve it.

"One of the things I strongly believe in, besides the values of taking risks and having fun while you do it, is that *what* we learn isn't as important as the learning itself. The most important thing we can learn is *how* to learn. The techniques and skills that we work so hard to acquire will soon be obsolete. We are doomed, in life, to learn skills that will constantly cease to be important or required. Today's skills will always be superseded by tomorrow's skills. Learning *how* to learn new ones is more important than *what* you learn.

"I think risk taking for a company, any company, is essential. If you don't risk, you don't grow. If you don't grow, you don't change. If you don't change, you die. However for a company to survive, there's a certain amount of conservatism you have to display. If you aren't conservative when it comes to seeking out and taking projects that generate income, then you risk closing your doors forever. And that's not the kind of risk you want to take with your company.

"One of the corporate risks we took that worked out very successfully was with our animators. Someone had the idea that it would be more energizing for our creative staff to work ten-hour days four days a week. Even though it meant way more work for our producing staff (who still had to work five days a week), the producing staff fully supported the idea. When Erik Vignau brought the idea to Tom, he also supported it, because it meant greater freedom and flexibility for the creative staff. The organization adjusted to meet the needs of the creative team, not the other way around. That's the kind of risk you *want* to take with your company — one that improves the level of fun at work and the bottom line at the same time."

The very nature of Will Vinton's business is fun. Creativity of thought, ideas, and expression are all fun and exciting. The execution of those fun elements can, however, become overwhelming. "At the beginning of each project, the fun and excitement and possibilities are without limit," says Gayle Ayers, director of M&M's commercials. "It's truly the reason I wanted to be here. At start-up there are ideas flying left and right. Everyone has another suggestion, another way to look at something. When we get into production, however, there can be times when it's not fun — when we're dealing with deadlines, and the pressure to hit air increases hour by hour."

In case you're not familiar with the requirements and pressures of animation, let me lay out some numbers. One 22 minute segment of *The PJs* (that's how long a half-hour television show is when you take time out for commercials and network-related announcements) takes 60 days of pre-production, eight weeks of actual production by the animators, and then 60 days of post-production. Imagine how many opportunities there are to get off schedule in a six-month process that includes up to three dozen creative people! And every show has an airdate and broadcast time that is locked in stone. That's pressure.

"One of the things that contributes to people having fun here," Gayle continues, "is their ability to define their own space." With regard to their personal space, Sue Conklin, Communications Coordinator adds, "We have something called 'Walk About Projects.' Any individual can propose a project and secure approval for it. This allows them to do something that interests them — it helps them define their space. The project is given carte blanche. The Studio supports it, assumes co-ownership of it, and takes the lead in marketing it."

In addition to the personal space, physical space at Will Vinton Studios is also something that gets defined. The walls of the 150,000 square foot warehouse-like buildings are covered with art — drawings, photos, and paintings. A six-foot oil painting of Albert Einstein created in 20 minutes by a performance artist hangs in Will Vinton's office. Sets, and prototypes of sets, are displayed seemingly on every horizontal surface available, likewise foam and clay characters of every imaginable sort — human form and otherwise! Walking through the Studios is a visual testimony to the fun that people who work here have.

Every wall I saw had artwork on it except in The Cave. The Cave is a fifty- by forty-foot room that is totally dark except for the glow of computer monitors in cubicles that ring the outside walls of the room. The Cave is home, as you might have guessed, to the Studios' computer animators. And in addition to being dark, it's also quiet. Computer animation takes intense thought and concentration.

Sean Burns is one of the animator/directors who makes his home in The Cave. "This is a great place to work. We work on truly interesting and cutting-edge stuff. Plus I get to work on things that interest me. Each project is a new situation every time. We suggest interesting

twists, new ideas. We get to take risks. There's no fun, after all, in playing it safe. Besides, this isn't brain surgery. What could happen?"

Doug Aberle is a more traditional animator/director with 17 years experience. "I always wanted to do special effects. Will Vinton Studios was the only one who took a chance on me and here I am. I like working on our television programs. It's a collaborative effort in an extremely creative atmosphere. There really isn't anyone telling us what we have to do. We are allowed to interpret the script in an appropriate manner, as long it's fun.

"At the end of the day, you've never been so tired — or had so much fun! There's a lot of variety in working on a TV show. There's something different every day."

Mary Sandell, Executive Vice President of Production and Producer of *The PJs,* knows about variety. "I was trained to be a lawyer. That's what I went to school for. I was actually in practice for two years. But it wasn't interesting to me and I hated the adversarial role I had to play. So I quit and waited tables. Talk about taking a risk! I spent some time in the arts as a grant writer and doing marketing for the local ballet. But what I really wanted to do was work for Will Vinton Studios. I interviewed for months! I kept applying. Finally, I told them I'd apprentice for a fee that was less than I was making at the ballet. They agreed and here I am. One of the things I took advantage of was the Studios' educational benefits. As long as I was employed full time, the Studios would pay 75% of my education costs. So I took courses related to what I wanted to do — produce!

"Eventually I was given a shot because of my persistence, educational improvements, and a really good mentor. I've been here 12 years and now I sign off on everything.

"Production, by its very nature, has to be loose. There's a lot of wild, creative activity, a lot of fun. My job is to see to it that the fun maintains its creative level yet the project stays on course. I am the calming influence. I try to give our people the framework in which creativity can flourish. I give them a blank canvas and they go to work. If I am good at what I do, I insulate the creative staff from the administrative aspects of the business. And I think I do a pretty good job.

"Every day is a new day. I don't know exactly what will happen each day because the collaborative nature of film brings such diverse voices to the creation process. It's terribly rewarding and incredibly invigorating and stimulating. And there's always room for fun, for jokes. I truly enjoy the people I work with. Their youthful passion for their work reinvigorates me each and every day.

"I'm very clear now on who I am and that my energies should be geared to grow and learn. The future is happening to me now. I like having the bar just out of my reach."

In order to bring the bar a little closer in a corporate business sense, Tom Turpin elected to come to lead the company. He left Virgin Sound & Vision, part of the London-based Virgin Group, to become the President and CEO of Will Vinton Studios in 1997. "My charge," Turpin relates, "is to build and maintain an organization that runs on passion, accessibility, equality, and respect; to create a blend of art and business that will support this company into the future. We don't need a hierarchy that goes against what we do. We manufacture emotion. If everyone were running around here being fearful, it would be impossible to be creative. Our products are full of creativity and play, and that play is the manifestation of fun." Turpin's success can be seen in the fact that revenues have tripled, profits have increased, and Will Vinton Studios has gotten into the production of long-format projects (television programs and films) in a big way. Their wildly creative staff now has larger and more profitable areas in which to display its talents and have fun while doing it. By minimizing the company's financial risk taking, Turpin has helped maximize their opportunities for creative risk taking. He has a vision to build one of the real creative powerhouses in film and television of this next century. "The only thing cooler than achieving my goal would be to help a lot of other people achieve theirs too."

David Altschul, President of the Advertising Division, and a filmmaker for 18 years, perhaps best sums up the attitude of Will Vinton Studios. "Permission to risk-take is essential for a creative environment. We have that permission here. In fact it's encouraged. Creativity is one of the forms that fun at work takes, so we also have fun. Risk in this business means that we frequently accept an assignment, take a job from a client and assume the responsibility to produce it to high standards by a seemingly impossible deadline, before we know what's expected or what it's going to look like. In the construction business for example, an analogy would be to sign a contract to produce a home based not on a final blueprint but on a felt-tip marker drawing made on a cocktail napkin. Those are the kind of risks we take all the time because we have the confidence that we can perform and that something very interesting will emerge."

That's risk at its highest; that's fun at its best.

■

Update: 2006

Since my first visit to the colorful studios of the famous creator of Claymation, everything has changed.

Gone is the wire letter basket being lowered on a rope from the ceiling.

Gone is portrait of Albert Einstein.

Gone is The Cave with its unearthly glow of computer screens animating ideas and emanating emotions.

Gone are the artwork-covered walls.

Gone are the displays and mock-ups that covered seemingly every horizontal surface in the 150,000 square foot studio.

Gone is the studio.

Gone is the name Will Vinton Studios.

Gone is Will Vinton.

Since it appeared in the first edition of *Fun Works*, Will Vinton Studios has fallen victim not to natural disaster, not to national tragedy, not directly to the economic downswing that felled the dotcoms. No, Will Vinton Studios has fallen victim to something far more common, something more eternal. Will Vinton Studios was the victim of the only constant in business. Will Vinton fell victim to change.

To be fair, change did not spring upon Will Vinton Studios unbidden in the dark of night. The change that devoured Will Vinton Studios was created directly by Will Vinton.

As Will told me six years ago, to be successful, risk-taking needs to have an economic foundation, a balance. In today's terms, the soft science of creation and risk-taking has to be balanced by the hard science of good product, economic conservatism, and making a profit.

By 2003, Will Vinton Studios was losing money. Following 9/11, many companies immediately cut back on expenses. Advertising was one of those expenses and Will Vinton Studios, dependent on commercial products to generate revenue, was spending large amounts of time and energy planning long-range projects at the same time as they were producing relatively low-paying television programs. By risk-taking and expanding into feature-length formats, they had made themselves vulnerable in the short-term to the economic catastrophes that befell many businesses in the last quarter of 2001 and most of 2002.

To offset those shortfalls, Will sought economic help. That help came in the form of Nike co-founder, Phil Knight. But as is often the case, that help came with a price that was measured in terms beyond dollars. In this case, the price was ownership.

Like Vinton, Knight lived in Portland. Like Vinton, Knight was the founder of an internationally known company. Like Vinton, Knight loved the creative aspects of movies. Unlike Vinton, Knight had no personal knowledge of what it took to operate Will Vinton Studios or to make movies. But he had the money and time to find out.

Knight loaned Vinton the money needed to stay afloat and at the same time became a partner in and shareholder of the business. The initial money was quickly consumed by the continuing preparations for producing new products. When the money ran out, Knight bought out Vinton completely and took over the company.

A short while later, Vinton left.

A lawsuit followed and the old Will Vinton Studios became LAIKA Entertainment. Vinton retained the name Will Vinton Studios but calls his new business Freewill Entertainment. Both companies remain in the Portland area and both produce animated projects.

Interestingly, both find themselves embracing expansive thinking and risk-taking. And both find themselves in need of better balance between their soft and hard sciences.

LAIKA Entertainment has the support and extremely deep pockets of Nike founder Phil Knight. LAIKA, funded by Knight, is building a thirty-acre campus in Tualatin, an upscale suburban area outside of Portland. The complex will house several buildings devoted to computer-generated animation, an exercise facility, a cafeteria, office buildings, and a staff of 400. More specific-function buildings are planned. It is Knight's and LAIKA's intention to create a company that will soon challenge Pixar and Dreamscape for supremacy in the world of animated films. To that end, Knight has hired many well-known animators as well as producers and directors of recent animated movies.

The core of LAIKA's staff still consists of the employees from the original Will Vinton Studios. Thus, much of LAIKA's culture has historic roots. What is not certain, and never is during periods of change, is whether or not a culture will continue to exist, disappear completely, or morph into something else. If LAIKA Entertainment is to represent the Fun Works living laboratory of Expansive Thinking and Risk Taking, then it must develop its soft-science side to match its hard science skills. It will need to become and remain a creative, fun place to work. Dale Wahl, LAIKA's President and CEO greets new employees and describes the company's culture opportunities like this:

"We encourage employees to think outside the box. We don't have to work within the confines of the conventions of the industry; we have to think anything is possible. And we have to avoid becoming our own worst enemy thinking we have to do everything the LAIKA way; there is no LAIKA way. We live in a rapidly changing environment that requires us to constantly embrace change and try new things. We make a real point of fostering creativity.

Cultivating creativity is an integral part of our long-term success. The goal is to have a workplace that is challenging, productive, successful, fun, and personally rewarding."

With thinking like that, it looks like LAIKA will pick up where Will Vinton Studios left off.

Freewill Entertainment, Will Vinton's current animation studio, is already producing animated product. Given Will's history of character creation and development and his awards for past creations, including an Academy Award, Freewill Entertainment will no doubt be strong in the soft sciences of creativity and ideation. It is likely that the creative culture of the original Will Vinton Studios will find a rebirth at Freewill Entertainment. What will have to be cultivated to balance their strong soft sciences are the hard sciences of finances and project management, elements that Will admits he failed to handle well the first time. Will Vinton realizes that good ideas are no good if they are not under financial control, that the structure of the organization must be strong enough to support both the culture and the creativity. If Freewill Entertainment is to become a strong force in the world of animation, if it is to represent the Fun Works living laboratory of Expansive Thinking and Risk Taking, then it will have to have its soft sciences firmly supported by its hard sciences.

In this example of corporate change, the company I originally interviewed as the representation of Embrace Expansive Thinking and Risk Taking has split like an amoeba into two firms, each of which must grow for itself the element lost to the other.

The result of this story is in reality another beginning. Where there was once one company in this Fun Works living laboratory, there are now two.

This is a story where both companies could grow. Or where both or either could falter and fail.

This is a story to watch.

■

The Journey vs Destination Key

ONE WAY TO EXPAND OUR THINKING is to look at life as a journey, not a destination. When we travel to a destination, we usually have a schedule, a deadline, a departure time, an arrival time, a pre-determined mode of transportation, and so forth. Not much is left to chance. When you travel to a destination, you know fairly well what you will see and when you will see it; you know what you will eat and when you will eat it. When you go on a journey, your travel is filled with unexpected experiences: you see things you never imagined; you eat things you never thought about eating; you learn things you never knew existed.

When you look at life as a journey, you look at life as a process. You know where you eventually want to wind up, you just don't know for sure how you're going to get there, when you're going to get there, or what you're going to do along the way.

After reading *Fun Works*, you may decide to integrate fun into your company's culture. Keep in mind that a company's culture is not rigid but is ever growing, ever changing. That it is not meant to be learned but is meant to be lived. Because culture changes, the best way to integrate fun into it is not to treat fun as a destination but rather, as a journey.

When you consider fun a destination, your charge might be: 'What we're going to do is make this company fun!' When you consider fun a journey, your thought process would be: 'What do we want this company to become?'

When you treat fun as a destination, you have to schedule your fun and the best you can do is arrive on time. When you treat fun as a journey and you allow fun the freedom to exist, then fun happens when it's needed and you arrive exhilarated.

When you take your company on a journey, you invite all its members to participate — to bring their diversity to the mix. You create a salad made of several kinds of greens and unlimited vegetables and fruit.

When you consider life a journey, you take a long-term focus on your intentions; you celebrate and visualize. And you change. But most of all, you discover that fun automatically shows up when it's needed. That fun has its own schedule, its own form, and its own reason for being.

Expand your thinking. Take a journey. And your fun will never end.

∎

> "Laughter is the best medicine."
>
> THE READER'S DIGEST

11

PRINCIPLE ELEVEN
Celebrate

THERE IS NOTHING MORE FUN THAN THE CELEBRATION OF SUCCESS

Recognition of success is not enough; we must also celebrate it. What gets recognized gets repeated; what gets celebrated becomes habit.

If we are going to successfully integrate fun and work, then the celebration of success must also be integrated into the fabric of work. We know that individuals require praise and recognition. We are learning that celebration generates additional energy for future endeavors, that it fuels high performance and increases the opportunity for, and likelihood of, even more success.

Celebration is fun. Do not separate celebration from work or distance it by time or space. Reinforce the integration of fun and work by the process of celebration — celebrate at work during work. When used throughout the work process rather than only at the end, celebration will give fresh energy to the work.

The principles for the celebration of success are the same as those for integrating fun and work: give permission; challenge your biases; be spontaneous; value diversity; et cetera. Follow these principles to infuse your work with both planned and spontaneous celebration. Start simply. When a group does something significant, celebrate the accomplishment before moving on. Make the effort to catch and compliment people doing something right. Look for opportunities to celebrate and then seize the moment with celebration.

Don't shy away, celebrate.

Dance to the music.

■

"I've learned that no matter how serious your life requires you to be, everyone needs a friend to act goofy with."

ANDY ROONEY

American Skandia
We Celebrate All the Time

"Celebrate, celebrate.
Dance to the music"
— KOOL AND THE GANG

To get to American Skandia's corporate headquarters, I took the 5:20 train out of New York City's Grand Central Station, through rolling, green-forested countryside, to Shelton, Connecticut. Here, a few miles from the Atlantic Ocean, I discovered a Fun Works living laboratory of Celebration nestled amongst typical New England homes and classic stone fences.

American Skandia is a manufacturer and wholesaler of insurance and financial planning products and services to brokers and financial planners all across America. The parent company, Skandia, was started in Sweden in 1855 as an insurance provider. Today, it is the largest asset gatherer in the world of non-proprietary market-linked insurance products. Their business is not to manage your personal money, but to manage the people who do. Skandia's goal is to attract the best money managers and financial planners to use Skandia's services rather than for Skandia to create their own financial products in the hope that brokers will sell their client a proprietary product that will return commission to Skandia.

Skandia believes that customer service is what makes brokers remain their customers. To that end, American Skandia spends much of its time and effort creating and developing top-notch customer service. To do that, they need good people who are highly motivated and well trained. When it comes to their philosophy of hiring, Jan Carendi, the founder of Skandia and Chairman of the Board, says it best: "Here at Skandia, we hire for attitude and train for skills."

More than 130 years after Skandia's founding, American Skandia came to the United States to a marketplace that was saturated. "Before Skandia decided to open a division in the States," Ian Kennedy, Senior Vice President and Director of Customer Services told me, "they hired a consultant to do a market analysis. The result came back that the market was saturated with financial

American Skandia

Where To Invest

services products and with a strong recommendation not to expand to America.

"Jan Carendi felt that since our concept was so different and our execution would be better, we should take the chance. So we did. Obviously, the decision was a good one because we're one of the fastest growing companies, if not the fastest one, in our industry. For example, from 1998 to 1999 our staff sized doubled to more than 1,400 people, and we have some of the highest sales in the entire country, ahead of The Hartford and TIAA CREF. In that same period, the product availability for our clients increased from 19% of what was needed to service their investors to 86%. And that's growing every year.

"But how do *I* measure success?" asks Ian Kennedy, Senior VP and Director of Customer Service. "I measure success by how excited our people are when they come through the door to work each day. And from what I see and hear, I think we're one of the most successful companies in the country. I spent 27 years in a large, bureaucratic organization. And while it was a great training ground and I moved all over, by the end of each work day I wasn't very happy. It was a mean environment. People weren't friends, they weren't even happy. I don't think they even cared about the customers they dealt with all day long in spite of the big banner over the door that said, 'People Are Important!' That feeling just wasn't in their hearts.

"Then I met Wade Dokken, the CEO of American Skandia. I could sense something different. Here was a company whose philosophy came directly from the top, from Jan Carendi. Jan says, 'The fastest way to guarantee a pink slip in this company is to *not* have fun. If you don't have fun, that might affect our company and infect others.' That sounded like someplace I wanted to work, and Wade offered me this position.

"Before I made the decision to give up the private consulting practice I had started after leaving that huge company and make the move to Skandia, I asked Wade if he would have dinner with me and my wife. I trust my wife's judgment and I thought this company just sounded too good. After dinner my wife said to me, 'What are you waiting for? Go!' So I did and I'm really glad!

American Skandia University

"I was hired to create an environment that was high on personal growth for the development of energetic people. I believe that in any successful business, the people are the heroes. Skandia's culture is such that we take care in the selection of people. When it comes to key people, everyone is involved in the search. We look for common values. We ask ourselves the question, 'Is this someone I will enjoy working with?'"

In addition to enjoying working with each other, employees of American Skandia enjoy a great physical environment that makes every day at work enjoyable and as much like a celebration as possible. American Skandia is located in two buildings of a four-building business park. Amenities for the employees include three restaurants (from gourmet to burgers), a dry cleaner, gift shop, copy center, shoeshine stand, chiropractor, and a world-class gym complete with steam, sauna, and changing facilities far better than any spa I've ever been in! Each floor of the five-floor facility has a coffee bar that is more like a Starbuck's than it is like a coffee station. There's a blonde-wood, modern-art-shaped counter with stools, plus overstuffed chairs that encourage relaxation and sharing of information between co-workers. Walking around the offices provided me with innumerable opportunities to see American Skandia's culture at work and to realize that getting and training the right people is only the first part of Skandia's equation for success. The second part requires keeping those people. The primary method used is celebration.

Webster's definition of Celebrate is: "to make an occasion by engaging in a pleasurable activity; to honor or praise; to perform publicly and formally." Skandia takes advantage of all those opportunities to celebrate, and celebrate with, its employees.

Terry Martinsky, Senior Service Manager for the Northeast Team, says, "I just knew that Skandia is where I wanted to be. I had worked for a very large company in the industry and they *used* to be fun. Then something happened to the culture and the fun disappeared. Here, even the training is fun. There are always so many new people that everyone has compassion for the new person — it wasn't that long ago that they were new, too!

"And we celebrate all the time. We take our team members to the Blue Fish games, that's our local minor league baseball team. If we're going to be working through lunch or dinner, we order in. To celebrate achieving our goals, we have catered breakfasts and lunches. And often, celebrations just happen. People who've worked late on a project decide to go out to dinner together after work. When you have good people, they like to be together and they like to praise each other and be praised.

"We have a tradition in our team called the Holiday Tree. Carolyn Jones, one of our team members, decorates a small, artificial pine tree in a theme to celebrate whatever is the next holiday (St. Valentine's Day, Halloween, Fourth of July) and puts it on a small table that she decorates with place mats and dishes that carry out her design. So every time you walk past Carolyn's celebration of the upcoming holiday, you smile and feel good, and you think about your *own* plans to celebrate it.

"Each team is always coming up with ways to celebrate the accomplishments of their team members. Sometimes those team celebrations become company-wide practices like our Warm Fuzzies."

Warm Fuzzies are 8½ by 11 computer-generated award certificates that congratulate a team member for team, individual, or personal accomplishments. They can be predictable or totally spontaneous but in both cases team members proudly display them on the walls of their offices where they can be seen while they're on the phone helping their broker/customers obtain the products they need to provide the best investment service for their clients.

The culture of American Skandia also allows for impromptu teams to form to deal with problems or situations. Recently, two new employees felt that the company's survival guide 'sucked' and proposed a re-write. Instead of getting uptight and defensive, the service managers to whom the idea was pitched told them to go ahead and redo it. The result was a web-based solution that far exceeded the original survival guide and which has become an internal benchmarking process for improvement. The creators, of course, were properly celebrated to ensure that what gets recognized gets repeated.

The most prestigious, externally generated benchmarking and reward system at American Skandia is the Dalbar. Dalbar is to the financial services industry what J.D. Power is to the airline and automotive industries — the benchmark that tells the world how good you really are. "Our goal," says Karyn Ebreo, Quality Assurance Liaison, "is to be Number One in Customer Service. Our job in Quality Assurance is to train and coach all the Reps; that includes Marketing Support Reps who handle the inbound telephone calls, Acquisition Reps who set up new contracts, Exchange Reps who set up new accounts that are transferred from other carriers, and Disbursement Reps who handle liquidating accounts. We also review one telephone call per week per Rep, and provide monthly feedback to the team.

"Dalbar regularly makes Mystery Shopper calls pretending to be a potential financial services customer. Based on the individual Reps fulfilling the criteria of Dalbar, American Skandia then disseminates awards to those who qualify." The Dalbar criteria for excellence include: Knowledge, Sales Appeal, Accommodation, Attitude, and Security Check. Not everyone receives an award for Dalbar excellence, nor is a Dalbar award necessarily awarded during each rating period. A Rep's interaction with customers must exceed the standards. In keeping with their core philosophy of rewarding behavior they want repeated, American Skandia presents Dalbar recipients with a plaque, a check for $500, their photo and story on the internal web, and dinner for the entire team. Winning a Dalbar is a high personal honor, an honor that's celebrated by and with the entire team.

In addition to the Dalbar, American Skandia created a monthly award called the STAR. The individual who garners the STAR receives $100 and their team $500 toward dinner. To further promote service excellence, the QA team created a challenge based on monitoring and scoring criteria developed by the Reps themselves. Individual scores are tied to each team and teams which maintain a 2.7 out of a possible 3.0 receive Hawaiian shirts, another form of celebration that goes a long way toward improving results and ensuring future behavior.

Yet another celebration program employed at American Skandia was called Reach the Peak. Reach the Peak celebrated the individual's contribution to helping the team reach its yearly goals. How? A watch worth several hundred dollars was delivered to the home of every employee at Christmas time!

This overriding concern for maintaining the competency and motivation of its employees is best expressed by Lars-Eric Peterson, President and CEO of Skandia. "Without motivated and competent employees, we will never be able to offer the best solutions in the market. Without satisfied and loyal customers, we will never be able to achieve long-term profitability. And if we cannot satisfy the shareholders who have invested money in our operation — if we cannot run a profitable business — then, ultimately we will have lost all joy in our work. It all hangs together."

"It all comes down to believing and trusting in people," says Wade Dokken, CEO of American Skandia. "You have to trust people if you want them to succeed. Then you need to reward them. We celebrate success by giving credit to others. I love people so it isn't really all that difficult. To be successful, you need to share and give power freely. It's our role to make them powerful."

An example of the kind of giving Wade is talking about was brought home to me by the story of Ian Kennedy and his assistant, Loretta Wieler, who switched offices. When Loretta was in the front space, there were a lot of disturbances and interruptions; once Ian was in front, the disturbances and interruptions seemed to disappear. For *both* of them! Now Ian sits out front in the smaller space and Loretta sits in back with the larger space!

When employees care more about each other's abilities and needs than they do about their own, when they praise each other for their successes, when your company has grown from new-kid-on-the-block to a market leader in slightly more than 10 years, then you must be doing something right. That's what's happening at American Skandia.

And that makes it fun to celebrate.

Update: 2006

When the hard science fails, not even the strongest and best of the soft sciences can keep a company from suffering.

This is what happened to American Skandia – a crisis of hard science. Throughout its sixteen-year history, American Skandia was a great place to work. Employees enjoyed their work and it showed. The soft science of Celebrate was at its best, rewarding ever-increasing sales, ever-increasing profits. The problem that befell American Skandia was not one of execution, it was one of planning, at least according to industry analysts.

American Skandia had made its reputation in the creation and marketing of variable annuities. In the late 90s, the market began to trend away from variable annuities toward fixed annuities. Because of its previous and immediate successes, and because of a corporate inclination, American Skandia did not attempt to balance its offerings with a strong line of fixed annuities, a product that does better in a poorer economy. American Skandia remained bullish on the future and reinforced their position on the bull-market loving variable annuity.

When the economy worsened following 9/11, American Skandia took a hit accumulating significant exposures to guaranteed death benefits, and found all its financial investments firmly lodged in the basket of variable annuities.

At that moment, Prudential (Fun Works living laboratory of Hire Good People and Get Out of the Way) found itself with ready capital generated by its IPO and a need to expand into the variable annuities market. Rather than create the products and support company themselves, Prudential began to search for a company to acquire. Because of American Skandia's great heritage and previous track record, coupled with the fact that its corporate culture matched up well with theirs, Prudential put in a $2.1 billion offer that was accepted.

"The human race has only one effective weapon — and that is laughter."

MARK TWAIN

Today, American Skandia is known as Prudential-American Skandia and its performance, supported by the diversity of products already offered by Prudential, helps their new parent firm be a leader in variable annuities in the United States.

In addition to retaining its name, at least in a hyphenated version, Prudential-American Skandia maintains the same culture of Celebrate that helped it earn its role as a Fun Works living laboratory. Employees still celebrate their success spontaneously and with planned programs. They still use DALBAR to evaluate their performance and they still celebrate their achievements.

The Holiday Tree also remains, as do the coffee bars where employees share with each other their successes on a daily basis.

In the face of their hard science disaster, American Skandia's soft science, its people skills, were strong enough to allow Prudential to see them as a balanced company that would flourish under new management.

And so American Skandia became Prudential-American Skandia.

And both companies celebrated.

■

"Where your treasure is, there will your heart be also"

MATTHEW, CHAPTER SIX, VERSE TWO

The Heart Key

CELEBRATION IS HOW WE SHOW RESPECT for a job well done; it's how we honor the individual who has accomplished good work. To ensure that celebration is authentic, it must show respect. And respect can only come from the heart.

In the past, we haven't felt comfortable bringing the full force of our emotions to our work, including our heart. Today, we talk about following our passion, about doing what we love. We are discovering that the best work is done with our head, our hands, *and* our heart. We are used to bringing our head and hands to our work, but to make our work complete, we need to bring our whole self — and that requires that we bring our heart.

The best conduit to our heart is fun. Fun makes work enjoyable, it makes us love what we do. Fun connects to love through the heart. When we enjoy what we do, we say we love our job. When our work is a 'labor of love,' it's less work and more fun. The more our work is fun, the more we love our work. The more we love our work, the more success we have. To ensure more success, we need to celebrate. Celebration requires heart.

Celebrate success with respect. Be authentic. Bring your heart.

■

"Work like you don't need the money.
Love like you've never been hurt.
Dance like there's no one looking.
Happiness is a journey not a destination."

PART THREE
Activating the Fun/Work Fusion

"Change does not necessarily assure progress,
but progress implacably requires change."

HENRY STEELE COMMAGER

CONCLUSION
Opening Our Minds and Letting Fun Happen

During one of the final travel sessions for my research on *Fun Works,* I found myself facing one of those interminable layovers that are built into some flights. I was sitting in a waiting room in the Houston airport with nearly one hundred other passengers in anticipation of our flight to Seattle, armed only with a list of things to get done and a book I could read if I finished my to-do list. Since I was on business, I was dressed in a serious business suit, carrying a laptop computer, a travel bag, and a large purse. I found myself seated next to a middle-aged man and woman whom I gathered from their dress and carry-on bags were both on business, too. The focal point of our wait was a group of nineteen-year-olds who apparently were traveling as part of an event for their church or their school. Unlike their staid traveling companions, these adolescents were seated casually on the floor, playing cards, laughing, and singing — obviously enjoying themselves, oblivious to the boredom and stress the rest of us were feeling. Impressed by their irreverent response to the situation in which they found themselves, I turned to my two fellow travelers and asked them when the last time was that they felt like that. They said they couldn't remember. When I asked them if they ever felt like that at work they simply smiled wistfully. But when I asked them,

"Wouldn't it be *nice* to feel like that at work?" they enthusiastically said, "Yes! Yes, it would!"

Several months later, I was again impressed by irreverence. This time it was during the closing ceremony for the Sydney 2000 Olympics. There, amidst serious-looking preparations for closing speeches, marching band performances, and banner-waving routines, was a grounds keeper on a lawn mower driving through the assembled celebrants, doing his job —

merrily mowing the lawn! "Leave it to the Aussies," I said affectionately as I laughed at the wonderfully irreverent image on the screen.

As a teenager, I spent a year as an AFS student in Australia. Since then, I have always felt I have Australia in my pocket, that my experiences have become permanently part of who I am and how I think and behave. One of the most important things I feel I have assimilated from that year's experience is the irreverent Aussie attitude. In Australia, they have a saying, 'Don't get too tall for your poppies,' which exemplifies their universal belief that it's not good to take yourself too seriously. That's what the image of the man on the lawn mower was telling us: these are only games, they should be fun. Don't take them too seriously, have fun with them. Enjoy the moment.

Needless to say, this Olympic reminder of Aussie irreverence immediately struck a responsive chord deep in my soul and helped me crystallize my attitudes about how we can best reintegrate fun and work.

AT THIS POINT IN A BOOK, THE AUTHOR OFTEN lays out a dozen or so action steps you can follow to implement his or her premise into your life. But I'm not able to do that, for if the reintegration of fun and work is truly to be successful, systemic, and long-term, then it needs to be integrated in a way that works for each person and for each company. That means that we need to change not how we *act* so much as how we *think*; that it is not about *changing what we do* so much as it is about *changing who we are*. Fun is not an artificial action or a set of beliefs that can be adopted. Fun must be woven into the fabric of the individual, the team, and the organization. Fun is not a set of new clothing that makes you feel momentarily more confident but rather a part of our DNA that is interdependent and deeply embedded.

Action plans create methods and rules for behavior; there is no action plan that will change how you think. And for fun to be successfully reintegrated with work, we are going to have to change how we think.

But that doesn't mean this message is without hope! There *are* things we can do that will help us open up our minds and let fun happen when it will.

FIRST, BE IRREVERENT. Challenge and question your self-imposed attitudes about fun and work. Be honest with yourself and look objectively at your opposition and resistance to changing those attitudes. Try to discover your *real* objections and determine if those objections are valid or merely 'the way you've always done it!' In business speak, being irreverent is often called 'thinking outside the box.' This means to not let the structure limit the ideas. What it means *effectively* is for you to question *what* you are doing, rethink *why* you are doing it, and be confident enough to laugh and smile when it feels like the right thing to do — regardless of the established protocol, regardless of the potential fallout. Even a bad situation can have a positive result.

I once had a client who became disenchanted with me when I sprayed him with aerosol confetti during my presentation at a Board of Directors meeting. Now if that sounds like a totally inappropriate thing for me to do, keep in mind that my reason for being at the meeting was to quickly and effectively engage the board in planning how to help the staff effectively manage the huge change that was about to happen in their day-to-day operations. I decided the best way to do this was to create a metaphor. I came to the meeting dressed once again in a serious business suit. This time, however, I had a tool belt around my waist. In that tool belt was a magic wand to create new futures, squirt guns to battle idea killers, Silly Putty® so they could stretch their thinking and skills, and Silly String® to celebrate their successes in a whole new way. I went through my entire tool belt of metaphors with the board to show them how I was going to make the employees look at change in a fun, new way — to see it as a more appealing situation rather than an impending threat. I did with the board what I would have done with the staff; it was behavior designed to help them become irreverent — to learn to think outside the box. While the president of the company was less than receptive to my presentation, the board members had a blast, immediately getting in on the fun by embracing the metaphorical tools and adding their own. The board members got it, the president didn't.

The positive result of this situation for me was that I discovered that my effort to bring effective change to the staff members of this company was going to be stonewalled at every turn by a man who thought there was only one way to behave at work — by a man who clearly thought that fun had absolutely no place in a working environment! It quickly became clear to me that the president of this company was not going to let me do the job for which I was hired. We ended the relationship and I replaced the client with one who valued irreverence, who was entirely open to change, and who asked me what he could do to make the process easier!

Irreverence may have a price. That price may be success deferred.

One of the things that became clear to me during the process of creating *Fun Works* was that successful companies, especially the young ones, have honest irreverence for things that truly don't matter. For them it's not important what you wear to work as long it's clean and properly covers your body parts. It's not important to many of them the hours that you work. What does matter to all of them is that work is fun, that you bring your whole self to work, and that you achieve and create the best results of which you are capable. The focus of these successful Fun Works Living Laboratories is not on the rules but on the result. They truly believe that fun works.

SECOND, SMASH THE MOLD. If the hierarchy is preventing change, change the hierarchy. If the rules prevent you from installing a new way of behaving that will improve results, change the rules. When businesses first start, there are no rules, there are no requirements except to succeed. As a business grows and gets older, both its successes and failures become examples of what works for them and what doesn't. Eventually, these successes and failures become rules written in stone — when this happens, never do this; when that occurs, always do this. Ultimately, a business born of new ideas and absolute freedom becomes burdened with restrictive attitudes and rules. So, when it's time for change in a business, often the first things to change are the rules.

Rituals, also, are extremely important for both human beings and companies. Like rules, rituals in and of themselves are neither good nor bad. The object is to not let rituals dictate what can and cannot be changed. Make your rituals positive, expansive ones not negative, restrictive ones. Keep the good ones, smash the bad.

THIRD, SLOW DOWN. You're moving too fast. The rush, rush, rush that we feel we must be part of, that we must pay homage to, is not necessary. In the course of the day, notice what's being said. Find the humor in the situation. Recall a previous anecdote and relate it. Take time out for lunch away from your desk. Go to dinner with your workmates both with and without spouses and significant others. Slow down and enjoy life.

The first time I went to Sedona, Arizona, I discovered a fabulous petroglyph in a cave. To me, it looked like a DNA strand so I created my own scenario of its origins, meanings, and implications that was totally unrelated to any facts whatsoever. I made it my person symbol. Some years later, I took my mother on vacation to Sedona. Like the good businessperson I am, I had created a schedule and timeline that would ensure we could get to all the important sites I wanted her to see. When we got to the cave, we only had a few minutes to spend or we were going to get off schedule and miss seeing something I can no longer remember, but which at the time I was certain was extremely important to visit. In my rushing to stay on schedule, some sort of disconnect occurred between my eyes and my brain. I knew I was in the right spot to show her my DNA petroglyph, the new symbol for my life, but I could not see it! I looked and looked and it was not there. My mother, sensing my anxiety but not displaying any of her own, simply looked where I thought it should be and said, "There it is, dear." And it was. I was rushing to get to a future time when I should have been living and enjoying the present one. Make this moment fun.

FOUR, LIBERATE YOURSELF FROM YOUR IMPOSED BEHAVIORS. As illustrated in the Timeline of Work Attitudes (pages 6 and 7), our attitudes about work are not absolute, immutable laws. They change with the prevalent attitudes of society. Therefore, you are not required either legally or morally to hold any opinions, attitudes, or behaviors about work that don't, so to speak, work for you. Because our society has isolated fun from work doesn't mean you need to do the same. Discard your belief that fun is silly and unprofessional; it simply isn't true. What is true is that work need not be 100% serious to be effective and profitable. Rebel against fear of change and against powerplays designed to thwart change or alter an environment that encourages it. The old ways and their supporters are strong; they are not necessarily right, just strong.

When you liberate yourself from imposed behaviors, you will discover the joy of fun in work. You will realize that success isn't the result only of dispassion, control, and power and you will come to the understanding that fun works.

There is still a kid in each of us, the infamous 'inner child.' Let yours out; let it play. Enjoy all facets of your personality. They make your work fun.

FIVE, MAINTAIN BALANCE. Excess is too much, even when it comes to fun. In the course of making changes, be careful not to eliminate 100% of the old and replace it 100% with the new. Don't eliminate the fundamentals, just blend them with fun. Fun can be either structured or spontaneous. Spontaneity, in fact, requires structure or it can't by definition be spontaneous. Work needs fun; fun needs work. In the perfect symbiotic relationship, fun makes work valuable, enjoyable, and profitable. As the old saying goes, don't throw out the baby with the bath water. Keep the baby; keep the fun.

THE OBJECTIVE OBSERVATIONS of the case companies in *Fun Works* support my original premise that business works best when fun and work are successfully integrated. The examples of the case companies give lie to the commonly held perception that there is no place in the working situation for fun; that the only time we can have fun is when the work is over; that the only way we can have fun is to earn it through hard work. In addition, these extraordinary companies have shown us that when fun and work are integrated, when companies embody the Principles of Fun/Work Fusion, the positive gains far outweigh any potential risks. These companies illustrate vividly that fun integrated with work:

- **Stimulates creativity and innovation**
- **Fosters commitment and ownership amongst all members of the organization**
- **Creates and secures the morale of their employees**
- **Impacts productivity positively**
- **Counters the effects of stress**
- **Acts as a vaccination for burnout**
- **Becomes the glue for social relationships**
- **Mends conflicts and heals hurts**
- **Stimulates renewal and activity**
- **Reduces absenteeism**
- **Creates stronger, deeper, longer-lasting customer relationships**

In addition, these companies are able to attract and retain peak performers in an economy that promotes and rewards the rapid and constant changing of jobs. This alone should convince you that fun works!

In short, the success of these companies who embody the Principles of Fun/Work Fusion can be seen in the financial strength of their respective organizations as well as in the positive attitudes of their employees. For these eleven companies, it is abundantly clear that fun works. And it works well.

NOW THAT YOU HAVE SEEN HOW ELEVEN COMPANIES successfully integrate fun and work, what more do you need to know to convince yourself to change your behavior and attitude toward work? What more to convince yourself to act on your instincts?

What bias do you need to challenge?

What habits do you need to change?

Once you have answered those questions, ask yourself this one: 'What would make it more fun to work here?'

You will be surprised at your response.

Fun works.

■

"The natural flow of the universe is abundance, joy and happiness."

Conclusion: 2006

As the last pages of this, the second edition of Fun Works, were being written, I once again found myself in the Houston Airport. I was walking down concourse B on my way to Concourse E, chuckling as I recalled our pilot's landing announcement: "Welcome to Houston Intergalactic Airport." One of the good things about flying with a connection through Houston is that I don't have to do a full workout when I get home. Walking between gates in Houston can be arduous work.

As I walked down, I could tell immediately that I was in Houston. Perched on top of his shoeshine box was man dressed in ironed jeans, shiny cowboy boots, and a black cowboy hat. As two businessmen passed him he called out to them, "Hey, pardners. Welcome to Houston. How about a shine before your meeting? Looks like you'all could use one."

The men smiled but politely waved him off. When I got even to the cowboy shoe shine man, I smiled and said, "Don't I get a greeting, too?"

As quick as a lariat brings down a calf, he said to me, "How's your day going, pretty lady? Welcome to Houston."

I said. "My day's going great, thank you, kind sir."

With that exchange of pleasantries he touched his hat and I nodded my head and we both smiled and continued on our separate ways. But we had each changed the other's life a bit and made our own a little nicer.

Exchanges such as that have become commonplace for me in the last six years as I travel the country, consulting with businesspeople on how to improve their soft sciences, strengthen their company's culture, and create sustainable organizations. I have tried to bring into my everyday life the lessons I know to be true in business. No longer is success determined simply by our ability to be smart and strategic. We need to create environments which resonate with the workforce, places that are fun to work, situations that fuel deep relationships. So I say hello to as many folks around me as I can. I smile a lot. I tell stories. I laugh. And I try to make everyone's life a little nicer place to be.

Well-being at work used to be a *nice to have*. When the first edition of *Fun Works* came out, it was hard for some to buy into the need for their organization to be as proficient in soft science as well as in hard science. But in a world filled with terrorists, and school shootings, and missing children, and a tight labor market, and changing technology, organizations have begun to realize that well-being at work is now a *need to have*. We still spend more time at work than at any other single activity and if companies are going to compete, survive, and thrive then our work experience must be a fun one. If organizations and the people who make them up are ultimately to be successful, we must balance them with strong hard science and effective soft science.

Is it still possible, some ask in the light of world realities, to think that we can and should have fun at work? To that question I answer, "Not only is it possible, it is a necessity."

If we as individuals, corporations, and even countries are going to compete, survive, and thrive, then fun at work is imperative. We know that fun at work works, that it is effective. We have seen the positive results in the case studies of the eleven companies in *Fun Works*. I, personally, have seen the Yin and Yang of hard and soft science work for hundreds more organizations world-wide.

When hard science is supported by soft science, then organizations are successful. When organizations are successful, they create a world that works for all.

To me, the answer is simple: fun works.

And it works over and over again.

■

PART FOUR:
Putting Fun to the Test

"I've learned that when you harbor bitterness, happiness will dock elsewhere."

ANDY ROONEY

The Fun/Work Fusion
Inventory

NOW THAT YOU'VE READ THE PRINCIPLES of Fun/Work Fusion and you've decided you'd like to better integrate fun into your work, what should you do? How do you know where to start? Remember it's not what you *need to do,* but instead what you are *being* that makes this fusion happen. Before you can make a successful plan of attack, you will need to have a good understanding of where you are and where you feel you can get to. One way to do that is to determine if you are behaving your way into a fun relationship with work by taking the following inventory and letting the results be your guide.

Each section of the inventory correlates to one of the Principles of Fun/Work Fusion. Put a circle around the number you feel best answers the questions in each section. Answer quickly, but honestly. Don't answer what you feel you *ought* to say (subjective), answer how things really are (objective). After you have determined your score for each section, transfer it to the Inventory Summary on page 201.

Now, re-read each section of the inventory and put a box around the number you think you could achieve *if you focused on that section with your full effort for 90 days.* Put your answer on the 90 Day Score line.

On the TFC line, enter the numerical difference between the two numbers. Do that for all the sections. TFC stands for Tension for Change. The larger the Tension for Change, the more improvement you feel you can make.

Start integrating more fun into your work using the principle with the largest TFC number. At the end of 90 days, shift your focus to the next largest TFC. Continue this process until you've gone through all the sections. Remember, this should be fun!

As you proceed, you will notice that even though you may be working on only one area of integrating fun in work, you are seeing improvement in several other areas at the same time. This is a concept known as 'all boats rise with the tide.'

Whether you choose to actively focus on increasing fun in work or not, the results of taking the inventory should give you a good idea of how successfully fun and work are integrated in your life.

Enjoy.

1

PRINCIPLE ONE
Give Permission to Perform

ALLOW PEOPLE TO BRING THEIR WHOLE SELVES
TO WORK EACH DAY

1	*2*	*3*	*4*	*5*
Never	*Hardly ever*	*Half the time*	*Most of the time*	*Always*

1. I welcome the whole person to the work, their ideas, interests and talent. 　1　2　3　4　5

2. I create time and space for conversations and discussion. 　1　2　3　4　5

3. I listen to and make each individual heard. 　1　2　3　4　5

4. I give and receive coaching and feedback. 　1　2　3　4　5

5. I embrace mistakes as opportunities to learn without blame. 　1　2　3　4　5

6. I forgive and forget and seek to grow from the challenges. 　1　2　3　4　5

Principle Score: _____

90 Day Score: _____

TFC Score: _____

The Fun/Work Fusion Inventory

PRINCIPLE TWO
Challenge Your Bias

REMOVE SELF-IMPOSED BELIEFS THAT ROADBLOCK
THE RELEASE OF YOUR FULL BEING

1	2	3	4	5
Never	*Hardly ever*	*Half the time*	*Most of the time*	*Always*

7. I challenge my own mindset and bias.   1   2   3   4   5

8. I share my information readily and broadly.   1   2   3   4   5

9. I proactively ready myself for change and practice flexibility.   1   2   3   4   5

10. I pursue and embrace out-of-the-box ideas and concepts.   1   2   3   4   5

11. I create as much latitude as possible for myself and others in doing the work.   1   2   3   4   5

12. I try new things even when I am fearful.   1   2   3   4   5

Principle Score: _____

90 Day Score: _____

TFC Score: _____

The Fun/Work Fusion Inventory

PRINCIPLE THREE
Capitalize on the Spontaneous

THIS IS NOT A PROGRAM BUT A PHILOSOPHY
IT'S NOT WHAT YOU DO IT'S WHO YOU ARE

1	*2*	*3*	*4*	*5*
Never	*Hardly ever*	*Half the time*	*Most of the time*	*Always*

13. I look for good intentions in others.   1   2   3   4   5

14. I don't create hierarchy to get things done.   1   2   3   4   5

15. I risk-take in taking action that is in alignment with our mission and values.   1   2   3   4   5

16. I champion the ideas of others.   1   2   3   4   5

17. I accept the responsibility to take positive action.   1   2   3   4   5

18. I hold myself and others accountable.   1   2   3   4   5

Principle Score: _____

90 Day Score: _____

TFC Score: _____

The Fun/Work Fusion Inventory

4

PRINCIPLE FOUR
Trust the Process

YOU CAN'T MUSCLE ENERGY
A LAUGH THAT IS FORCED IS NOT A TRUE LAUGH

1	2	3	4	5
Never	Hardly ever	Half the time	Most of the time	Always

19. I respect the efforts and contributions of all co-workers.	1	2	3	4	5
20. I maintain a posture of approachability and openness.	1	2	3	4	5
21. I stay informed on the process.	1	2	3	4	5
22. I support the sharing of power and information and work to minimize organizational politics.	1	2	3	4	5
23. I listen without judgment.	1	2	3	4	5
24. I strive to look at each situation with a fresh and open mind.	1	2	3	4	5

Principle Score: _____

90 Day Score: _____

TFC Score: _____

The Fun/Work Fusion Inventory

5

PRINCIPLE FIVE
Value a Diversity of Fun Styles

WE DON'T ALL DO IT THE SAME WAY

1	2	3	4	5
Never	*Hardly ever*	*Half the time*	*Most of the time*	*Always*

25. I remove obstacles that impede opportunities.   1 2 3 4 5

26. I understand and accept that different people have different needs and one is not right or wrong.   1 2 3 4 5

27. I support different types of expression.   1 2 3 4 5

28. I strive to create a space that is accommodating and flexible to different needs.   1 2 3 4 5

29. I risk-take in expressing my own ideas in my own way.   1 2 3 4 5

30. I maintain respect through listening openly to the thoughts, opinions, and ideas of others.   1 2 3 4 5

Principle Score: _____

90 Day Score: _____

TFC Score: _____

The Fun/Work Fusion Inventory

PRINCIPLE SIX
Expand the Boundaries

DON'T MAKE RULES THAT LIMIT THE PROCESS

1	2	3	4	5
Never	*Hardly ever*	*Half the time*	*Most of the time*	*Always*

31. I involve others in the design of projects and process.   1 2 3 4 5

32. I seek to include the voice of all team members, including
those of the customer and vendor partners.   1 2 3 4 5

33. I pursue my own development, learning, and growth.   1 2 3 4 5

34. I care about both the little and the large things.   1 2 3 4 5

35. I am clear on expectations (mission, values, measures).   1 2 3 4 5

36. I communicate my expectations to others.   1 2 3 4 5

Principle Score: _____

90 Day Score: _____

TFC Score: _____

The Fun/Work Fusion Inventory

PRINCIPLE SEVEN
Be Authentic

BE TRUE TO YOUR BEST SELF AT ALL TIMES
BE CONSCIENTIOUS

1	*2*	*3*	*4*	*5*
Never	*Hardly ever*	*Half the time*	*Most of the time*	*Always*

37. I accept responsibility for my own attitude.   1 2 3 4 5

38. I understand the impact of my behaviors upon others, including my co-workers.   1 2 3 4 5

39. I am willing to be challenged and challenge others on behaviors that are incongruent with goals.   1 2 3 4 5

40. I support the success of my co-workers.   1 2 3 4 5

41. I look for ideas to improve the way we do things.   1 2 3 4 5

42. I accept responsibility for my mistakes.   1 2 3 4 5

Principle Score: _____

90 Day Score: _____

TFC Score: _____

The Fun/Work Fusion Inventory

PRINCIPLE EIGHT
Be Choiceful

EMBRACE THE WHOLE PERSON

1	2	3	4	5
Never	*Hardly ever*	*Half the time*	*Most of the time*	*Always*

43. I start each day with renewing my commitment to myself, my co-workers, my organization, and my work. 1 2 3 4 5

44. I initiate actions that will improve relationships and outcomes. 1 2 3 4 5

45. I seek to provide positive solutions. 1 2 3 4 5

46. I share my fun self with others, including customers. 1 2 3 4 5

47. I assert my ideas. 1 2 3 4 5

48. I work to resolve issues that undermine our success. 1 2 3 4 5

Principle Score: _____

90 Day Score: _____

TFC Score: _____

The Fun/Work Fusion Inventory

PRINCIPLE NINE
Hire Good People and Get Out of their Way

TRUST YOUR EMPLOYEES TO USE THEIR JUDGMENT

1	2	3	4	5
Never	*Hardly ever*	*Half the time*	*Most of the time*	*Always*

49. I support an environment that creates the latitude for individuals to pursue their passion. 1 2 3 4 5

50. I embrace work that is challenging. 1 2 3 4 5

51. I foster collaboration rather than competition in completing work. 1 2 3 4 5

52. I seek to learn from others' experiences. 1 2 3 4 5

53. I value and celebrate my co-workers' talents. 1 2 3 4 5

54. I am open and honest in my communication. 1 2 3 4 5

Principle Score: _____

90 Day Score: _____

TFC Score: _____

The Fun/Work Fusion Inventory

10

PRINCIPLE TEN
Embrace Expansive Thinking and Risk Taking

LEARN HOW TO HARNESS AND DEVELOP
THE FULL POTENTIAL OF EMPLOYEES

1	2	3	4	5
Never	Hardly ever	Half the time	Most of the time	Always

55. I extend trust to my colleagues.   1 2 3 4 5

56. I am in touch with my intuition and use it as a guide.   1 2 3 4 5

57. I experiment and try.   1 2 3 4 5

58. I create room for possibilities in conversations and work.   1 2 3 4 5

59. I reserve judgment.   1 2 3 4 5

60. I assert my full talent each day at work.   1 2 3 4 5

Principle Score: _____

90 Day Score: _____

TFC Score: _____

The Fun/Work Fusion Inventory

11

PRINCIPLE ELEVEN
Celebrate

THERE IS NOTHING MORE FUN
THAN THE CELEBRATION OF SUCCESS

1	2	3	4	5
Never	*Hardly ever*	*Half the time*	*Most of the time*	*Always*

61. I capitalize on the spontaneous opportunities for recognition.	1	2	3	4	5
62. I am open to both giving and receiving praise.	1	2	3	4	5
63. I participate in the celebration of good work and high standards.	1	2	3	4	5
64. I contribute to making our work environment positive.	1	2	3	4	5
65. I share in the work load equitably.	1	2	3	4	5
66. I find new ways, both little and large, to celebrate our success.	1	2	3	4	5

Principle Score: _____

90 Day Score: _____

TFC Score: _____

The Fun/Work Fusion Inventory

FUN/WORK FUSION
Inventory Summary

	PRINCIPLE	90 DAY	TFC
PRINCIPLE ONE:			
PRINCIPLE TWO:			
PRINCIPLE THREE:			
PRINCIPLE FOUR:			
PRINCIPLE FIVE:			
PRINCIPLE SIX:			
PRINCIPLE SEVEN:			
PRINCIPLE EIGHT:			
PRINCIPLE NINE:			
PRINCIPLE TEN:			
PRINCIPLE ELEVEN:			
TOTAL SCORES:			

FUN/WORK FUSION
Inventory Scoring

INDIVIDUAL PRINCIPLE
RANGES

1 – 6	This principle is an external concept in your work life.
7 – 12	What obstacles or mindsets do you confront in wanting to use this principle?
13 – 18	How could you increase your consistency in the use of this principle?
19 – 24	You are consciously competent in this principle.
25 – 30	You have internalized this principle in your work life.

Was any one particular statement an area for emphasis for reflection/growth?

TOTAL SCORE
RANGES

1 - 66	You still think the horse and buggy is the best way to travel.
67 – 132	Start with principle Eight and explore your choicefulness.
133 – 198	Find and develop areas you have identified as opportunities for growth.
199 – 264	You are on your way to achieving Fun/Work Fusion. Continue the journey.
265 – 330	You are bringing your whole self to work each day. Share your spirit with others.

If you would like to take your organization's pulse, contact Catalyst Consulting Group Inc. for a Fun/Work Fusion Inventory Kit.
Catalyst Consulting Group Inc.

12701 Larchmere Blvd
Suite 4A
Cleveland, Ohio 44120
216.791.7802
216.791.7860 fax
fun@catalystconsulting.net
www.changeisfun.com

OTHER VOICES
Stories of Fun at Work

THE FOLLOWING AUTHORS regularly count on and benefit from the Principles of Fun/Work Fusion.

We have included their voices as examples that society's relationship with work is changing and that regardless of the kind of work you do, you, too, can successfully integrate fun and work.

As you read their stories, see if you can identify which of the Principles of Fun/Work Fusion they best illustrate.

May their voices give you courage on your journey.

■

Fun Is The Way We See Our World

Elizabeth Jeffries
President, Tweed Jeffries
Author of *The Heart of Leadership: How To Inspire, Encourage, and Motivate People to Follow You*

FUN KEEPS YOU SANE! It gives you perspective on how little control we have over the things that surround us, and yet, how much control we have within ourselves. Fun is the ability to laugh at ourselves. That's why people love jokes. They reflect the truth and make us laugh at events and happenings that could make us cry or would make us crazy if we didn't laugh at them!

When you have fun, you see life differently. Fun is a philosophy, the way we see our world, no matter the circumstances. It makes the big issues more manageable and we're able to get into solutions instead of getting stuck in the problem.

To integrate fun and work, encourage employees and give them permission to release their internal playfulness. Then encourage child-like behaviors such as trust, openness, and inquisitiveness, as opposed to childish behaviors such as pranks and silliness.

The organization needs to create a 'home' for people to bring the best of their whole selves to work each day and to let fun be part of their culture. Fun is the common denominator that gets people to be real.

To keep fun in your life, hang around people who have this philosophy: 'I will let no one rob me of my joy today.'

And then live by that philosophy.

■

Become Involved in the Process

Robert Fritz,
President, Robert Fritz, Inc.
Author of *The Path of Least Resistance at Work*

IT IS DIFFICULT FUNDAMENTALLY FOR WORK TO BE FUN if the work is not fair. If biased and preconceived results are expected, no amount of inner strength can make the experience fun or worthwhile. The fun/work dynamic is not a superficial distraction from reality, but instead, a deeper understanding of and involvement with the work. That's why work needs to align with your values if it is to be fun and worthwhile.

Fun means very different things to different people, and the differences come from personal temperament, personalities, values, aspirations, sense of humor, sense of irony, and sense of enjoyment. But one thing that is often true for most of us is that fun is a natural by-product of doing work that is aligned with our deepest values, and work that is meaningful and worthwhile to us.

For some people, fun comes from moments that are distractions from the harshness of reality. These moments help put life into perspective, and help us catch our breath, so that we can better deal with situations. But there is a deeper, and more encompassing aspect of fun, and that comes from the opposite of distraction from reality: it comes from true involvement with life, even when it isn't always pleasant. The deeper desire people have here is for involvement. They are looking for work that not only matches with their core values in life, and is therefore meaningful to them, but they are also looking for an opportunity to become involved in the process, to give of themselves. Sometimes this is fun — sometimes it is not.

Most of the time, I experience fun at what I do. And for those few times when I am not, I am busy trying to get there.

■

Be Inclusive, Not Exclusive

Chip Bell
Senior Partner, Performance Research Associates
Author of *Customer Love: Attracting and Keeping Customers for Life*

TO ATTRACT AND RETAIN TALENT, especially those under thirty, fun and work have to be wired together. Today's young employees are looking for more than a job, they want something that has a sense of poetry to it, they want to be involved in a noble cause and a quality journey. They are looking for work that is balanced with fun.

Companies that have this balance exhibit increased productivity, creativity, and innovation. In addition to being fun and playful, these organizations are more courageous, take more risks, and exhibit more growth.

If you want to stimulate fun, be inclusive not exclusive. Draw on the brilliance of your front line.

Be careful that fun becomes hard-wired into your culture and is not merely an add-on. Add-on fun is cosmetic and unsustainable. When fun is organic, it becomes the way we live and the way we think, and therefore the way we act.

The nature of fun is that it is spontaneous and free. It has a life of its own. It only needs an environment in which to grow and then it becomes the way in which we see the world. When fun grows in a culture, people smile, they laugh, and they succeed.

And they put more of themselves into what they do because they truly enjoy it.

■

Fun is a Process, Not an Event

Martha Finney
Co-Author of *Find Your Calling: Love Your Life*

WE WORK IN AN ERA WHERE PRODUCTIVITY and innovation are the competitive levers. To succeed, it takes people power which is fostered in an open, expansive environment. That fostering is what's fun.

I usually describe that fun as joy. I believe joy is a process, it is not an event. To me, fun is a fleeting experience, joy is the long-term result. Joy is being able to express the best of your whole self. It is the adventure of coming to terms with yourself as a player on this planet, complete with all of its highs and lows.

Coming to our fullness in our work is one of this era's greatest legacies. It has required courage, the ability to draw boundaries, and the understanding of the continuum of life, learning, and maturity.

Too often people confuse the perfect job with perfect work. We search for the perfect job but it doesn't exist. When we search for our mission, we discover our perfect work. If you would experience joy at work, then integrate fun, have hiring managers who truly believe you can find work that you love, be respectful of all individuals, become partners with employees to fulfill their futures and dreams, support them by cultivating their talents, and make the workplace abuse-free so they may safely apply their passions.

Joyfulness promotes a new way to discover the appreciation of the gift of life.

■

Turn Fun-Killers into Fun-Lovers

Bob Pike
Chairman, CEO
Creative Training Techniques International, Inc.
Producer of award-winning videos and
Author of *The Creative Training Handbook*

IT IS NOT A CHOICE BETWEEN FUN AND WORK, it is a choice *for* fun *and* work. I find it depressing that so many people spend 8 hours a day at work and 16 hours trying to forget that they did!

It's time for us to replace the common definition of work: if it is not dull and boring then it can't be work! Work should be about passion, it should have a sense of purpose, it should be about involvement and participation. High performing teams who do challenging work also know how to have fun. They have an attitude that says they enjoy what they do and that they belong to a diverse group of committed individuals who know the mission, values, and vision of the team. And they look forward to making a contribution.

Understand that there will always be both fun-loving and fun-killing people. Fun-killers don't actually object to the fun, they feel that the fun isn't relevant to the work and therefore not important. To turn fun-killers into fun-lovers, intentionally make fun relevant. No one can object if something is relevant, productive, *and* fun.

And look for a champion. Every cause needs a champion around whom to rally. Can't find one? Become the champion yourself.

It'll be fun!

Restrictive Environments Reduce Fun

Jerry Fletcher
President, High Performance Dynamics
Author of *Patterns of High Performance*

LAUGHTER IS A UNIQUELY HUMAN TRAIT. Laughter has a healing quality. Laughing allows us to soften the hard edges of reality and makes us feel better when we've finished.

Humor can juxtapose things so that we see them in a different way. And that different perspective allows us to gain insight. You can tell that someone has reached a deep insight into themselves and into their own behavior and thinking when they crack up laughing.

There is a synergistic quality to the sharing of fun, joy, and humor. It allows us to take chances, to dare. It compounds and increases our energy. It allows us to throw ourselves wholeheartedly into our work. And when we do, then fun is inherent as long as the work environment is supportive of the human effort. The more restricted and restrictive the environment, the more difficult it is to foster fun.

When things are working right and going well, there is strong sense of fun. When there is a strong sense of fun, things tend to work right and go well.

■

Fun Cannot Be Imposed

Alan Briskin, Ph.D.
Alan Briskin & Associates
Author of *The Stirring of Soul in the Workplace* and
Co-author of *Bringing Your Soul to Work:
An Everyday Practice*

FUN IS A COLLECTIVE, UNIVERSAL EXPERIENCE. It is not just one's personal arena. Fun tries to connect with others; it creates shared significance. Fun is the experience of the joy of which we are capable as humans. It is part of our nature.

Since fun is part of our lives, it is therefore intrinsic to work. Fun doesn't mean avoiding hard work or hard times. It means paying attention, practicing mindfulness, and looking for common ground with others. When we are overwhelmed, what we need to do most is see our situation clearly. Maintaining perspective, laughter, and yes, having fun helps us through uncomfortable situations. My mother once said laughter is the catharsis of the soul. I learned from her that shared laughter was like medicine, it heals the psychic wounds we all sustain in life.

Fun is about being open. We have to become less tight with ourselves and with others. We need to become vulnerable, to let go, to release control, to lean on each other, to allow ourselves to depend on each other. No easy task. Fun is the mechanism to achieve that. When we have fun, we are connected; when we are connected we have the true exchange, the give and take that is required for work to be as productive as it can be.

Fun cannot be forced or it becomes one-sided. Sarcasm is one-sided fun. It is limited and non-universal. Fun cannot be imposed on people or called up on demand, or quantified on a chart. To create an atmosphere where fun flourishes, listen to your inner self. Leave room for spontaneity. Be conscious of what you are doing at all times. Allow people to share their full selves. Give permission to tell stories.

And share yourself with others.

■

Why Haven't I Chosen Fun?

Dr. Lawrence L. Lippitt
President, Lippitt-Carter Consulting
Author of *Preferred Futuring*

FUN IS A DECISION. It is a decision to be joyful or not. You decide. Fun is where we have to go to improve the quality of our life; it is when we feel like we are making a decision. To see if you are having fun, ask yourself: 'What does it look like when I'm happy? Am I happy now? Am I having fun? If not, why haven't I chosen fun?'

When it comes to work, we are up against our mental models of joy vs. toil. We believe that work is toil and cannot be fun. This mental model presents an important question for each individual to address, one which is actually a spiritual problem.

What do we know about fun and work? We know that people who incorporate fun and work live better and are more creative. We know that where there are highly cooperative systems, there is more fun and productivity; that collaborative relationships lead to deeper understanding and improved results.

The joy that comes from good work, comes naturally. Bringing joy into the workplace means connecting with one's passion. The key to shifting energy in a positive way is to tap into your passion. To bring fun and joy into your company's culture, listen to the heart and truth of your employees, tap into their passions, and shift the culture from control to involvement.

Make it your goal to make a difference. If you do the right things, fun, joy, and meaning are the results.

The Team that Plays Together, Stays Together

Gail Howerton, M.A., CLP
CEO (Chief Energizing Officer), Fun*cilitators
Author of *Hit Any Key to Energize Your Life*

LIFE IS TOO IMPORTANT TO BE TAKEN SO SERIOUSLY. Many things measure our lives: career, relationships, education, families, wealth; and each of them is connected to who we are and where we come from. To make these aspects of our lives better, we need to look for the humor in them, appreciate that humor, and get a daily dose.

Most of us seem to listen to that oldies radio station WII-FM, better known as 'What's In It For Me?' We become self-centered, then jaded. And when we get to the point that we don't care, then our soul dies. To avoid this unhappy ending, learn to facilitate fun. Fun is the liberation of talent, it is the end of restraint by rules. People need to know they matter and make a difference. Fun brings everyone into the process, gets them involved, and reinforces their value to the team. And the team that plays together, stays together.

You need all the members of your team to become involved but remember, you can't force the process or it's not fun. The fun culture must be sincerely supported by management, yet it must allow for innovation. You'll know fun is working in your business when your employees have ownership. When fun is sincere, they will buy in to it and fun will become automatic.

■

Fun Promotes Teamwork and Cooperation

Mel Silberman, Ph.D.
President, Active Training
Author of *PeopleSmart: Developing your Interpersonal Intelligence*

FUN IS NOT A MEANS TO AN END. You don't decide to use fun to get what you want, fun is a way of behaving. A fun approach often opens a door that creates a deeper understanding, that intensifies the positive results of a discussion.

One of the advantages of fun in the workplace is that it's hard to have fun by yourself, you need other people to have the best fun. Fun, then, promotes teamwork and cooperation. Fun is an attitude of playfulness that promotes experimentation and enhances creativity. It creates a sense of vitality and relieves competitive pressures. Fun helps to maintain flexibility in a changing environment. Fun is 'business as unusual.'

On the personal level, fun creates the flow between an individual and their humanity. Fun keeps us connected to who we really are; it makes us realize that we are all in this together.

■

Love What We Do

Laurence D. Ackerman
Senior Consultant, Team Leader
Sigelgale
Author of *Identity is Destiny*

THE SINGLE MOST IMPORTANT NEED WE HAVE as individuals is to work in an environment that celebrates, rather than minimizes, the human element. It is very difficult to have fun when our humanity, our individuality, has been diminished.

Over the last century, the field of scientific management has contributed to the extraction of the human element by arguing that people are emotional and thus inefficient; i.e., fun at work is dangerous. Today, there is still a profound distrust of fun by many managers. Why? Because we have been trained that work must be serious and deliberate to be important. If it is fun, it is not serious, therefore it is not important. We must see the flaw in this assumption and fight it.

In my experience, companies who succeed at having fun celebrate what they do and who they are. As a result, fun is embedded in the culture rather than mandated through picnics, Nerf® ball contests and softball games. The payoff is that there is a strong natural alignment between an employee's personal identity and the identity of the organization.

From a recruiting, training, and development perspective, it comes down to a simple philosophy: Love what we (the company) do and do what we love. If both parts of this mandate are genuinely fulfilled, fun at work is nearly assured.

Living this philosophy is also the only road for celebrating the human element which draws upon our unique strengths, validates our identity, and leads us to freely invest the best of ourselves in an organization.

Have Fun: Become a Sage

Dick Richards
Organizational Consultant
Author of *Artful Work: Awakening Joy, Meaning,
and Commitment in the Work Place*

WHAT IS FUN AT WORK? To me it's being with the right people — people whose work I respect and whose egos are not getting in the way of doing important work. I enjoy being able to hang out with people who demonstrate this kind of respect.

When I work with a client and we get to the end of the project, I feel great about the work we've accomplished; and in the process, I discover, I have an enormous amount of fun. Why? Because the relationship worked. It's always a joy to realize that great work and fun are not incompatible and that if I've done it once, I can do it again.

All I have to do is follow a few rules:

1. **Keep it simple.** Don't try too hard, don't make it too complicated. The best songs often have easy melodies.
2. **Stay in tune.** Pay attention to what's going on around you. Observe the state and status of everyone involved.
3. **Know when the energy has become negative.** Even when things start out well, there are always times when they go bad. Say, 'This doesn't feel good. Can we change it?' And then do.

When things are fun, you can feel the nuance and the commitment of another in each other's success. I try to follow this advice from the Lakota Indians: 'A sage is someone who enjoys life and then tells others about it so they can have the experience.'

■

Am I Getting Paid to Do This?

Janelle Barlow
President, TMI USA
Co-Author of *A Complaint is a Gift*

THE ACID TEST FOR HAVING FUN IS: 'Oh, man! And I'm getting paid to do this?'

If you maintain the mental model we all seem to have been born with of work first, then have fun, then work, then fun, you may never determine yourself worthy enough, or accomplished enough, to deserve the fun. In other words, we seem to follow some rule that says fun is a reward that we are allowed to experience only after we have worked hard enough to earn it!

We need to shift to a mental model in which the work itself can be intrinsically fun if we find work that connects to who we are and what we want to accomplish in life. Then fun exists at the same time as work. They are interrelated and joy is the result.

Fun isn't necessarily laughter, but it is the enjoyment and fulfillment that comes during and after the work process. But the work process definitely is easier when there is laughter and fun.

When we have ownership of our work, we can release our full commitment to it and invest our full selves. And when we do, fun and joy follow.

■

Put Your Arms Around Fun

Cathy Fyock
President, Innovative Management Concepts
Author of *Get the Best: How to Recruit
the People You Want*

FUN IS NOT AN ESCAPE FROM WORK, it is a value shared with team members. When there is agreement surrounding core values, individuals free their potential to perform. Likewise, work is not drudgery. Work can and should be intrinsically enjoyable.

There are two levels of fun in the workplace: applied activities and internal attitude. The deeper fun occurs when you give of yourself, when you are achieving a greater good. It's the sense of fulfilling one's purpose. Experiencing this deeper level is what truly makes work fun.

When an organization embraces the deeper level of fun, it manifests its sense of purpose and its set of unifying values. This, then, creates the framework for individuals to release their energy, and experience the satisfaction and joy of adding value to the structure of work.

Doing work that one is well suited for, and using one's God-given talents, creates joy. If you get excited about work, you are igniting the human spirit in others. To encourage individuals to put their arms around fun, we must get beyond superficial measures, embrace the whole person, and give people permission to follow their hearts and dreams.

The organization which can do this, which can capture the human potential and look beyond the numbers, will find and keep the hearts of their employees.

■

It's Hard to Have Fun Alone

James M. Kouzes
Chairman Emeritus, tompeters!company
Co-Author of *The Leadership Challenge*

HOPE AND OPTIMISM ARE THE CORNERSTONES of commitment and long-term success. In order to sustain hope and optimism over time, you need to find the balance between work and fun.

Why? Because when work is not fun, it becomes drudgery, which leads to physical and mental anguish, and to poor health. When work *is* fun, it's good for your health, you feel better and perform better. Healthy employees are more satisfied and more likely to contribute and to be successful.

It's hard to have fun alone. Social connectedness fosters fun and fostering fun creates happiness and good health.

There are seven essentials to fusing fun and work:

1. **Take charge.** Don't wait for fun and life to come to you, seek out fun. Proactive people are happier and get more out of life. It takes courage but the risk is worth the reward.

2. **Expect the best.** Set the standards high. Have a strong belief in the ability of others to meet those standards. Expect the best from people and you will be rewarded.

3. **Be observant.** Actively seek out people who are living the standards and values of your company. Tell their stories broadly. Celebrate and recognize them in a genuine way.

4. **Arouse your own positive thoughts.** Make fun your idea. If you think it's fun, and it's kind and gentle, do it.

5. **Express hope.** Hope is not a passive condition. Hope is having the will, and knowing the way will follow. Hope requires action.

6. **Offer love and encouragement.** The more you give the more you get. Make it your priority to support; seek out those who need it.

7. **Set the example.** If you are living to your standards, walking your talk, you will quickly be seen as credible and genuine; if not, people will know you don't mean what you say.

■

Fun Is Not a Sugar Coating

Sivasailiam Thiagarajan
President, Workshop by Thiagi, Inc.
Author of *Thiagi Game Letter: Seriously fun activities for trainers, facilitators, and managers*

AMERICANS TREAT WORK IN A SCALLOP MANNER. We believe that life must either be work or fun, one first then the other. We try to achieve a balance between work and fun, not too much of one nor too much of the other. We have artificially separated fun from work.

A better way to live life is to blend choices, to find a way to have fun and work together, at the same time. Fun, when truly blended in our lives, transcends time and space, it acquires a life of its own.

To be successful at blending fun and work, we must remove the negative baggage associated with fun. Fun is not sugar coating, it is not applied. Fun does not have work as its opposite. We are not required to work hard in order to earn our fun. Sometimes when people are having fun, a guilty feeling kicks in. They think to themselves that if they continue to have this much fun, they will have to pay for it later. Bring fun elements to the things that aren't fun. If you can change a situation, change it; if not, change your attitude towards it.   We have lost the ability to have fun that we had when we were babies. Babies are totally hedonistic about fun — they know how to have fun.

Living fully is to embrace all dimensions of life: joy and pain, fun and work. The goal in life is to learn to take serious things lightly and lighten things serious.

Blending fun and work is the first step.

■

To Make Fun Happen, Make Choices

Dorothy Marcic
Author of *Managing with the Wisdom of Love*

EACH OF US EXPERIENCES FUN DIFFERENTLY, depending on our sense of purpose. Fun is linked to having a clear purpose and responding to it, and to the experiences that come with pursuing that purpose. Fun is the feeling we get from the positive impact of our contributions.

Alfie Kohn, author of *No Contest* said, "When you have a competitive system, the only person who feels good is the one who wins." Fun is not exclusive, it is holistic. It is the combination and connectedness of work from the head, heart, and hands. It is not fun when there is a lack of respect and generous spirit; that squelches creativity. When there is arrogance, exclusion, and unbending hierarchy, there is no fun for anyone.

To make fun happen, we need to start making choices. Do I do it because I have to or because I want to? When you have discovered your calling and you are driving that passion, everything you do is innately fun. It doesn't mean it isn't work, that you don't work hard — you do, probably harder than you did before. I'm convinced this experience is what gave birth to that old cliche: 'Time flies when you're having fun.'

If you're tired of doing stuff that isn't fun, touch your heart and theirs, help people change.

■

Creating Games Improves Results

Alan Gregerman
From his book *Lessons from the Sandbox,* ©2000
Published by Contemporary Books.

WHATEVER YOUR PRIORITIES ARE, take another minute to think about the role of play in improving your results. At first glance you might see how having more fun could improve teamwork, morale, and spirit in your workplace. But that's just scratching the surface. Remember that kids learn by playing and incorporate play into everything they do.

What about developing a game that helps your people improve production or service delivery? What about injecting play and humor into efforts to attract the best employees or energize customer service? Maybe the right starting point for your company is simply to commit to testing the values of play.

Begin by asking people across the organization to identify specific opportunities to interject fun into their work activities and space. Then try some of their ideas.

■

Fun is Learning from Bad Ideas

Charles Decker
Co-Author of *Beans: Four Principles for Running
a Business in Good Times or Bad*

YOU CAN THINK WHAT YOU WANT about the dot-coms, but I've never had so much fun in my life! In my opinion, fun is giving people the right tools to do their jobs well, and empowering them to make mistakes and learn from bad ideas. At Amazon basically anything goes. It's so refreshing to have people say: 'try it and see what happens; if it doesn't work, we'll take it down.'

The hiring bar at Amazon has always been extremely high. They hire the best people and get out of their way. The diversity factor is incredible here. The amount of encouragement for different styles of work is amazing. For example, yesterday it was a beautiful day in Seattle, and several people said that they were going out to enjoy the sunshine. They didn't need any managerial sanction, and others said that more people should go out and do this. I've been in so many companies where they have organized programs to have fun at work that seem so phony to me. It was almost like a chore to go and have a brownie because it was so fake.

I think Amazon has done a brilliant job of getting the best people. I've been in rooms where I feel like I'm the dumbest person there. People are given the chance to do what they do best, and they are given the tools to do their jobs well. After 20 years in publishing, I have to say that's rare.

Doing a good job, being professional, making money, all of that is fun for me. That to me is authenticity. I'm a merchant, and my celebration is when the cash register rings. When the customer is thrilled, getting what they want, that's the celebration for me.

■

Like a Bunch of Bad Little Kids

Judith A. Neal, Ph.D.
Director, Center for Spirit at Work
West Haven CN

IN MY FIRST PROFESSIONAL JOB I worked for Honeywell on an organizational development consultant team. Part of our philosophy was to have fun together because we really believed it would enhance our work. Once we had to prepare a major presentation for the VP of Human Resources about our plans for the next couple of years.

There were eight people on the team from HR and one engineer. So while we were all being kind of crazy and spontaneous and out of control with the pressure of what was going on, the engineer was sitting at the table methodically thinking through what had to be done. I noticed that he was quietly folding a paper airplane. I sat down next to him and copied what he was doing, because I didn't know how to make paper airplanes very well. Pretty soon more people were making paper airplanes and we all started throwing them around the office.

One of the airplanes glided out the door and down the hallway. We all ran to the door and saw the airplane land on the VP of HR's doormat! Our mouths dropped in horror because he might walk out any minute and that would be the end of our department — we were considered to be rather flaky! At first we sat there in shock, then we started egging each other on about who was going to go get it — like a bunch of bad little kids!

So finally I said OK I'm going to get it. I ran down the hallway, picked it up, and ran back with my prize. Everyone cheered! It was so silly and so funny, with just this little element of risk that we would get caught doing something that you usually wouldn't expect to see in a corporate setting.

Within twenty minutes everything in the presentation fell right into place. There was something about that spontaneity that caused a shift from the high pressure, heavy, 'we've got to work this through,' to 'we're confident that what we're doing is of value and makes a lot of sense.'

The VP loved our presentation. We were able to implement a major new change initiative in the corporation. It was outstandingly successful.

■

Fun is Losing Your Self in Your Work

Joel Suzuki
President, Star Throwers
Producers & Distributors of Training Videos

IN HAWAII, WHEN OUR EXTENDED FAMILY goes to the beach, the children swim and the aunties sit on lawn chairs, never taking their eyes off the children all day long. At the end of the day, when the sun settles over the mountain and the children are in the car, one of the aunties makes her way to the water's edge. Cupping one hand to her mouth, she calls to the ocean, "Children, time to go." With a gentle wave of her hand, she calls out each of their names, then returns to the car.

In our family we believe when a person has fun, the inner child is released. By calling out their names, the inner child and the person are once again united.

May you find your work to be such good fun that at day's end, someone calls out your name.

■

"The true object of all human life is play. Earth is a task garden; heaven is a playground."

G.K. CHESTERTON

ACKNOWLEDGMENTS

I did not invent or discover the connection between meaningful work and the experience of joy; the relationship is as old as work itself. Nor am I the 'Queen of Fun.' I, too, battle with my own chronic intensity. I am a person like others, traveling a path in the pursuit of using my talents to the greatest advantage and good. On this path I have discovered that my wellspring of joy comes from helping others realize their true potential and release it into the world.

Capturing my learning in book form represents the contributions of many individuals without whose invested talent and commitment this endeavor would not have been as much fun nor the outcome as uplifting.

BERRETT-KOEHLER PUBLISHERS for believing in the value of my work and creating a better world through publications.

STEVEN PIERSANTI for helping me crystallize the principles which gave me focus.

RANDY MARTIN for being my partner, my foil, my wordsmith, and my editor.

SUSAN MARTIN for the necessary but tedious work of copy editing.

STEPHEN CALHOUN and members of the Catalyst Consulting Group team, for their constant support and presence.

DICK RICHARDS, BJ HATELEY, TOM BROWN, BARRY OSHRY, JANIELLE BARLOW, BERNIE DEKOVEN, AND DENNIS & MICHELLE REINA, the Berrett-Koehler family of authors, for sharing their stories.

THE CASE COMPANIES for opening their doors and letting us inside.

THE YERKES FAMILY, MY PARENTS JIM & BETSI, MY SISTER JANE, HER HUSBAND JIM, AND THEIR DAUGHTERS ERIN, COURTNEY, AND LINDSAY; MY AUSTRALIAN FAMILY, THE LEONARDS; MY SWEDISH FAMILIES for being my source of inspiration, joy, happiness, and fun; AND MY NEW BROTHER FRED, known as Captain Fun to his coworkers.

And MY CIRCLE OF FRIENDS, too numerous to name, for being there when I needed them.

Thank you all for helping *Fun Works* become real a second time.

Leslie

■

"Play is the exultation
of the possible."

MARTIN BUBER

INDEX

"What is work? and
What is not work?
are questions that perplex
the wisest of men."

BHAGAVAD-GITA

FUN/WORK FUSION
RESOURCES

THE FOLLOWING SUPPORT MATERIALS ARE CURRENTLY AVAILABLE TO ASSIST YOU
IN CREATING AN ORGANIZATIONAL CULTURE WHERE FUN ENERGY EMERGES IN THE WORK

THE FUN/WORK FUSION EXPERIENCE

A highly interactive process designed to assist organizations to enliven their culture with the Fun/Work Fusion principles. The multi-session process includes a pre- and post-climate survey, a motivational kickoff keynote, 11 half-day experiential learning experiences staged to engage individuals in the practice of each of the 11 Fun/Work Fusion Principles while promoting individual performance, teambuilding, innovation and trust.

FUN/WORK FUSION INVENTORY

A simple assessment providing feedback to individuals, teams or the organization as to whether their behaviors create the climate for fun to coexist with work in a productive manner.

CUSTOM KEYNOTE ADDRESSES

Energize your organization with a fun presentation that sparks their desire to bring the best of their whole selves to work each day.

To learn more about how to create a culture infused with fun and which sustains performance please contact us at:

Catalyst Consulting Group Inc.
12701 Larchmere Blvd
Suite 4A
Cleveland, Ohio 44120
216.791.7802
216.791.7860 fax
fun@catalystconsulting.net
www.changeisfun.com

We would love to hear your stories of how your organization
integrates fun into the work with improved results.

"Work is something you want to get done; play is something you just like to be doing."

HARRY WILSON

LESLIE A. YERKES

LESLIE YERKES IS PRESIDENT of Catalyst Consulting Group, Inc. (www.changeisfun.com) an organizational development and change management consulting firm based in Cleveland, Ohio. Leslie's business goal is to help people create sustainable organizations. Her life goal is to create a framework in which people can draw on their own resources to find creative solutions. Her clients have included Chrysler Corporation, The Cleveland Clinic Foundation, United Church of Christ, International Steel Group, Mittal Steel USA-Cleveland, and NASA. A subspecialty of Leslie's is making non-profits healthy and sustainable.

Leslie is a recognized consultant, author, and speaker throughout the United States and Europe. She is considered an expert in her field and is frequently quoted in the media. She is the coauthor of the bestselling *301 Ways to Have Fun at Work, Beans: Four Principles for Running a Business in Good Times or Bad,* and *They Just Don't Get It! Changing Resistance into Understanding.* Her works have been translated into more than a dozen languages selling hundreds of thousands of copies world wide.

A graduate of Wittenberg University and Case Western Reserve University, she has taught at John Carroll University and Baldwin Wallace College. She is on the faculty at the Weatherhead Dively Center of Executive Education and the Mandel School of Applied Social Sciences, Case Western Reserve University.

■

ABOUT
BERRETT-KOEHLER PUBLISHERS

BERRETT-KOEHLER IS AN INDEPENDENT PUBLISHER dedicated to an ambitious mission: Creating a World that Works for All.

We believe that to truly create a better world, action is needed at all levels — individual, organizational, and societal. At the individual level, our publications help people align their lives with their values and with their aspirations for a better world. At the organizational level, our publications promote progressive leadership and management practices, socially responsible approaches to business, and humane and effective organizations. At the societal level, our publications advance social and economic justice, shared prosperity, sustainability, and new solutions to national and global issues.

A major theme of our publications is "Opening Up New Space." They challenge conventional thinking, introduce new ideas, and foster positive change. Their common quest is changing the underlying beliefs, mindsets, institutions, and structures that keep generating the same cycles of problems, no matter who our leaders are or what improvement programs we adopt.

We strive to practice what we preach — to operate our publishing company in line with the ideas in our books. At the core of our approach is *stewardship*, which we define as a deep sense of responsibility to administer the company for the benefit of all of our "stakeholder" groups: authors, customers, employees, investors, service providers, and the communities and environment around us.

We are grateful to the thousands of readers, authors, and other friends of the company who consider themselves to be part of the "BK Community." We hope that you, too, will join us in our mission.

BE CONNECTED

VISIT OUR WEBSITE

Go to www.bkconnection.com to read exclusive previews and excerpts of new books, find detailed information on all Berrett-Koehler titles and authors, browse subject-area libraries of books, and get special discounts.

SUBSCRIBE TO OUR FREE E-NEWSLETTER

Be the first to hear about new publications, special discount offers, exclusive articles, news about bestsellers, and more! Get on the list for our free e-newsletter by going to www.bkconnection.com.

PARTICIPATE IN THE DISCUSSION

To see what others are saying about our books and post your own thoughts, check out our blogs at www.bkblogs.com.

GET QUANTITY DISCOUNTS

Berrett-Koehler books are available at quantity discounts for orders of ten or more copies. Please call us toll-free at (800) 929-2929 or email us at bkp.orders@aidcvt.com.

HOST A READING GROUP

For tips on how to form and carry on a book reading group in your workplace or community, see our website at www.bkconnection.com.

JOIN THE BK COMMUNITY

Thousands of readers of our books have become part of the "BK Community" by participating in events featuring our authors, reviewing draft manuscripts of forthcoming books, spreading the word about their favorite books, and supporting our publishing program in other ways. If you would like to join the BK Community, please contact us at bkcommunity@bkpub.com.